P9-CCR-760

What's the Difference?

What's the Difference?

How Men and Women Compare

Jane Barr Stump, Ph.D.

William Morrow and Company, Inc.
New York

Grateful acknowledgment is made for permission to reprint information from the following sources:

What Women Want by Caroline Bird. Copyright © 1981 by Caroline Bird. Reprinted by permission of Simon & Schuster, Inc.

What Every Woman Should Know About Men by Dr. Joyce Brothers. Copyright © 1981 by Joyce B. Enterprises, Inc. Reprinted by permission of Simon & Schuster, Inc.

"Just How the Sexes Differ" by David Gelman, John Carey, Eric Gelman, Phyllis Malamud, Donna Foote, Gerald Lubenow, and Joe Contreras. *Newsweek*, 5/18/81, pp. 72–83. Copyright © 1981, by Newsweek, Inc. All Rights Reserved. Reprinted by permission.

U.S.: A Statistical Portrait of the American People, edited by Andrew Hacker, assisted by Lorrie Millman. Copyright © 1983 by Andrew Hacker. Reprinted by permission of Viking Penguin, Inc.

Men: A Book for Women, edited by James Wagenvoord. Copyright © 1978 by Product Development International Holding, n.v. Reprinted by permission of Avon Books, New York.

Women: A Book for Men, edited by James Wagenvoord. Copyright © 1979 by Product Development International Holding, n.v. Reprinted by permission of Avon Books, New York.

Library of Congress Cataloging in Publication Data

Stump, Jane Barr.
What's the difference?

1. Sex differences—Dictionaries.   2. Sex differences (Psychology)—Dictionaries.   I. Title.
HQ9.S78   1985   305.3'03'21   84-20569
ISBN: 0-688-04192-2

Printed in the United States of America

First Edition

1 2 3 4 5 6 7 8 9 10

BOOK DESIGN BY JAMES UDELL

WITH LOVE FOR

Ann and Don

Tommy and Judy

Bill and Wanda

Bill and Jeanette

Bob, Chris, and Margaret

My father and in memory of my mother

Foreword

We live in a time of great identity confusion. Our descendants may look upon our age, shake their heads, and wonder how we survived at all. Hopefully, they will view our divorce rates (one-half of all marriages end in divorce), our loneliness, our suffering, our ignorance of the essential male and female, and our lack of wisdom, with a sense of sadness and compassion because they will know more about what we all need to know: who we are and what it means, first, to be human, and, second, to be male or female. They will know how to utilize that knowledge to enhance the quality of life, to love with vitality and honesty, and to enjoy what we all seem to long for: a sense of intimacy with our mates that is met with awe, gratefulness, and a security and peace that "passeth understanding," as well as an opportunity to enjoy a commitment to one's life's work that is steeped in excitement, change, challenge, and fellowship with those of like mind.

This book does not intend to try to give the reader that great knowledge of self that is held for the future. It does hope to give a synopsis of the data currently available on the physiological and social differences between American men and women in the hope that some of the confusion that is so prevalent will be dissipated. All of the entries are accompanied by references so the reader can pursue further information.

The information in this book has been gathered from sources published since 1975, with some exceptions, including such classics as Jacklin's and Maccoby's *The Psychology of Sex Differences*, Bernard's *The Future of Marriage*, Frankfort's *Vaginal*

Politics, and Money's and Ehrhardt's *Man and Woman, Boy and Girl,* and various medical and psychiatric textbooks. It must be understood that the information is general rather than specific. Many of the findings quoted here are contestable, and the reader will find that the results of some studies contradict those of others. There are, of course, innumerable individual differences between men and women, and this presentation certainly does not pretend to be the absolute truth. It is meant, rather, as a guide for us as we continue our quest for who we are, and for the freedom that can rise from that new sense of identity.

—JANE BARR STUMP

Acknowledgments

I would like to acknowledge the invaluable help of my friends and colleagues Irving Marvit, M.D., John McCarthy, M.D., and Gail Marcus, with gratitude for the wonderful conversations, the consultations, and their loving support during the writing of this manuscript.

I wish to acknowledge my sister, Ann Weems, also a writer, for her continued support, excitement, humor, and love expressed in innumerable letters and phone calls from St. Louis to Honolulu. Her support was wonderful and life-giving, and to her I express my thanks and ongoing love.

My agent, George Taylor, provided invaluable guidance, technical expertise, and a caring attitude that has proven invaluable. To him, I give my thanks.

And lastly, I would like to acknowledge and thank Kristina Lindbergh, the editor of this book, for her gracious support, her enthusiasm, the sharing of herself, her marvelously warm letters, and her excellence as an editor. To her, I owe a great debt.

—JANE BARR STUMP

Abdomen
The abdomen is the part of the body located in the space between the chest and the pelvis. According to the results of a 1976
West Point male/female comparative study, the strength of the
abdominal muscles are the same in both men and women. A
woman's abdominal muscles are more elastic and flexible than a
man's so that her abdomen can swell in pregnancy.
(*Hammer, p. 21; Marvitt, M.D. [interview]; Brothers, p. 23*)

Abortion, Spontaneous (Miscarriage)
More males than females are spontaneously aborted.
(*Dranov, p. 22; Segal, p. 29*)

Abstract Reasoning and Intelligence Quotient (IQ) Tests
Women usually score slightly lower in the part of an IQ test that
involves picking out a visual pattern hidden in a maze. Some
authorities believe this is the result of conditioning. Others attribute it to brain differences.
(*Star, 6/21/83, p. 22*)

Abuse of Children
Males: Forty-two percent of child abusers are males.
Females: Forty-eight percent of child abusers are females.
(*Bird, p. 96*)

Accessibility of Managers in Business World
Males: Male managers are less accessible than female managers.

They have their doors closed more often and have their secretaries screen staff requests for conferences more often.
Females: Female managers are more accessible than male, and leave the door open twice as often. They tend to leave their offices to see if everything is "okay" and encourage weekend and evening calls as well as interruptions by staff.
(*Researcher: Jatasha Josefowitz, College of Business, San Diego University*)

Accidental Deaths
Male: In 1977, 71,935 men died accidentally.
Female: 31,267 women died accidentally.
(*Almanac, 1981; p. 140*)

Accountants
Forty percent of the accountants in the U.S.A. are female.
(*Kantel, p. 11*)

Achievement Tests
Girls between the ages of nine and seventeen lag slightly behind boys of the same age in standardized test scores, even though they reach physical and mental maturity earlier. Many feel this is a result of cultural conditioning.
(*Segal, p. 29; Safran, p. 12*)

Achievers, Low
(Those who do not perform according to their abilities.) Boys outnumber girls as low achievers.
(*Sexton, p. 74*)

Acne
More men than women have acne. This is because men have higher levels of the hormone testosterone, which stimulates the sebaceous gland to produce more of the fatty substance that clogs the pores and causes infections.
(*Pascoe, p. 88*)

Acting Schools
Women outnumber men in acting schools.
(*Bird, p. 88*)

Activity Limitation Due to Chronic Conditions

Male: There are 15.5 million men whose chronic conditions limit their activity.

Female: There are 15.9 million women whose chronic conditions limit their activities.

The most common limiting factors are:

Condition	Male	Female
Heart disease	18%	14.7%
Arthritis or rheumatism	11%	23.7%
Hypertension without heart involvement	7.7%	12.1%
Impairment of back and spine	9.1%	9.2%
Impairment of the lower extremities and hips	9.0%	7.1%

(The less-common conditions vary considerably.)

(Statistical Abstract of the United States, *1981; p. 121*)

Actors and Actresses, Television (1977)

There are more roles for men on television than there are for women. According to a Screen Actors' Guild study, there are seventy actors for every thirty actresses. In children's programs, there are two men for every one woman.

(*Bird, p. 88*)

Adam's Apple

Only men have the protruding bulge in the neck called the "Adam's apple." This is due to the outward projection of the expanding larynx, which is stimulated by male hormones called androgens.

(Woman's Body, *p. 414*)

Adrenaline Levels When Under Stress

When a person is under stress the body releases a number of hormones that cause such reactions as a rise in blood pressure, an acceleration of the heart beat, and a slowing down of digestive activity. One of the hormones responsible is called adrenaline or epinephrine. It has long been thought that the adrenaline level rose faster and higher in males than in females. However, in a study that tested the adrenaline levels of female bus drivers and female engineering students, it was shown that their adrenaline levels rose as rapidly as did those of males, so it is speculated that the social roles people play may influence the levels of this hormone under stress.

(*Bricklin, p. 77; Hammer, p. 24*)

Adultery and Divorce
In the United States, adultery on the part of the female is more likely to lead to divorce than is adultery on the part of the male.

(*Anderson, p. 96*)

Aerobic Power
(Meaning literally "with air," aerobic refers to one's capacity for oxygen uptake.)

After age twelve, males have from 15 percent to 30 percent more aerobic power than do females, due to a greater lung capacity, a higher hemoglobin count, and a higher metabolic rate, all of which allow more oxygen to be carried in the red blood cells. However, in a test involving top runners of both sexes, it was found that after intense training, the aerobic capacity of the females was only 4.3 percent lower than that of the men.

(*Klafs and Arnheim, p. 184; Ross, 1981, p. 24*)

Age, Median
The median age of males is 29.3 years.
The median age of females is 31.9.

(*U.S. News & World Report, 11/29/82; p. 54*)

Age, Median at First Marriage
In 1980 the average male had been married at the age of 24.8.
Women had married at an average age of 22.3.

(*Almanac, p. 784*)

Age and Marital Status
Male: One fourth of men age sixty-five or older are divorced, widowed, separated, or were never married.
Female: Almost two thirds of all women over sixty-five are widowed, divorced, separated, or were never married.

(*Somerville, p. 112, 113*)

Age and Marital Status: Age 75 and over
Male: In 1981, 3.5% men were single; 72% were married; 22.1% were widowed; 2.5% were divorced.
Female: 6.2% were single; 23.3% were married; 68.2% were widowed; 2.3% were divorced.
   (Hacker, p. 30)

Age and Sex (1983 Census)

	Male	Female
Under age 5	8,360,135	7,984,272
5– 9	8,537,903	8,159,231
10–14	9,135,055	8,925,864
15–19	10,751,544	10,410,123
20–24	10,660,063	10,652,494
25–29	9,703,259	9,814,413
30–34	8,675,505	8,882,542
35–39	6,860,236	7,102,772
40–44	5,707,550	5,960,689
45–49	5,387,511	5,700,872
50–54	5,620,474	6,088,510
55–59	5,481,152	6,132,902
60–64	4,669,307	5,416,404
65–69	3,902,083	4,878,761
70–74	2,853,116	3,943,626
75–79	1,847,115	2,945,482
80–84	1,018,859	1,915,370
85 and over	681,428	1,558,293

   (Hacker, p. 30)

Aggression
Male: Men are more aggressive than women. Males of most species seem at all times to be more ready than females to fight physically and verbally. This is related to the higher levels of testosterone, a sex hormone, in the male body. Young men, for example, commit the majority of violent crimes at the age when their testosterone levels are at a lifetime peak.
   (Wagenvoord/Bailey, Women, p. 24)
Female: Women are less aggressive than men. When they do fight, they usually utilize verbal means. Although women have

testosterone in their blood streams, the levels are considerably lower than those found in men.
(*Wagenvoord/Bailey*, Women, p. 103, 104)

Aggression, Response of Nursery-School Teachers to

Nursery-school teachers respond three times as often to aggressive behavior, such as hitting or breaking things, in male than in female children. Boys usually receive a stern reprimand in a loud voice, whereas girls receive a soft reprimand.
(*Serbin and O'Leary*, p. 57)

Aggression and Children

Boys fight more than girls and often daydream about aggression. (The fighting can be observed starting at about age two.)
(*Wilson*, p. 50)

Aggressiveness in Work

Women are not as aggressive as men in pursuing their professional goals. Many feel this is both a biological and a cultural syndrome. Unlike men, women do not have high levels of the hormone testosterone, which stimulates aggressiveness. In general, they also have less training in aggression.
(*Wagenvoord/Bailey*, Men; p. 255)

Aging

Aging can be defined as a process in which the numbers of healthy cells in the body decline.

Men age faster than women.

Women age much more slowly than men except in the case of skin, because the skin of a woman is thinner than that of a man.
(*Brothers*, Woman's Day, 2/9/82, p. 139)

Aging, Response to

Older women tend to deny aging, and respond to it with psychological stress. They become less involved socially, in contrast to older men, who tend to accept aging, become more involved in community activities, and are much less likely to report psychological stress.
(*Atchley and Seltzer*, p. 289)

Aging and Capacity for Exercise
Male: A man's capacity for exercise drops 10 percent for every ten years of age after the age of twenty. A man of sixty has 60 percent of his twenty-year-old capacity.

Female: A woman's capacity to exercise drops only 2 percent every ten years of age after twenty. A trained woman of sixty can exercise up to 90 percent as hard as she could at twenty, and a forty-year-old woman's capacity is very close to that of a twenty-year-old.

    (Brothers, Woman's Day, 2/9/82, p. 139)

Aging and Employment
Males: In 1979, 20 percent of men over sixty-five remained in the labor force, in contrast to 45.8 percent in 1950.

Females: In 1979, 8.3 percent of women over sixty-five were in the labor force, in contrast to 9.7 percent in 1950.

    (Hacker, p. 120)

Aging and Effectiveness of Ova and Sperm
Male: The sperm produced by an older man are quite capable of impregnating a woman.

Female: The ova that remain in the female ovaries at menopause are not thought to be "old, defective eggs" but rather undeveloped ones. The "genetic time clock" prevents the follicle-stimulating hormone from signaling the egg to mature, so it fails to do so.

    (Wagenvoord/Bailey, Women, p. 176)

Aging and Hormonal Decline
Male: Testosterone levels decline in a man at the rate of about 1 percent per year until, at sixty or so, its level is about that in a nine-year-old boy, but impregnation is still possible.

Female: The decline of ovarian estrogen at menopause is reduced to about one quarter to one third of what it was during the menstrual years. This dramatic decline occurs during the first year or two of menopause.

    (Wagenvoord/Bailey, Women, p. 176)

Aging and Income
Males: In 1981 the median income for males in their fifties was

$20,956. For men sixty-five or over, the median income was $8,173.

Females: The median income for women in their fifties was $6,067. The median income for women sixty-five or older was $4,757. (The poverty level for people sixty-five or older living alone is $4,359.)

    (Somerville, pp. 112, 113)

Aging and Personality Changes

Older males become more submissive, whereas older females become more assertive and dominant. Sexism is less prevalent, as men become more tolerant of their increased interest in family and in nurturing, and women become more accepting of the role reversals, and of their own assertiveness.

    (Mitchell, p. 168)

Aging and Poverty

The poorest people in the country are old women. Their median income is about $4,757, or about half the income of men their age.

    (Somerville, p. 112)

Aging and Sexual Activity

Sexual activity is possible for the elderly of both sexes as long as they are in good health, although some medications can decrease desire or cause impotence in males. Authorities indicate that sexual activity is good for health as it lubricates the sexual organs and adds to a feeling of self-esteem and of being loved.

    (Cooley, pp. 307–311)

Aging and Sexual Arousal

It takes longer for both sexes to become sexually aroused as aging progresses. After sixty, a woman may need 1 to 3 minutes of sexual stimulation for adequate lubrication to occur. Between the ages of fifty and seventy, a man may find that an erection takes minutes rather than seconds.

    (Kart and Manard, p. 206; Health and Longevity Report, Vol. 2, p. 3; Cooley, p. 310)

Agoraphobia
(Agoraphobia is a fear of open places, of crowded places, or any situation in which one cannot escape quickly.)
Ninety percent of agoraphobic patients are female.
(Weekes, British Medical Journal, *1973; 2:469)*

AIDS: Acquired Immune Deficiency Disease
In AIDS victims, the immunity system weakens to the extent that a variety of debilitating diseases can occur. Of the 2,000 cases seen since June 1981, 82 percent have died. There are now seventy to eighty cases being reported daily. The cause of the disease is unknown, although some scientists speculate that it may be caused by a virus. The high risk groups are homosexual men, intravenous drug users, and hemophiliacs. The disease is thought to be transmitted primarily through sexual contact, and most of the victims range in age from twenty to fifty, although the disease has been known to strike children. Only 5 percent of the reported cases are female. Seventy-five percent of the cases reported are homosexual men.
(Barrett, p. 98, 100, 202)

Aid to Families with Dependent Children (AFDC)
In the United States, 4 million people receive funds from AFDC, and 93 percent of those are women and children.
(Ehrenreich and Stallard, p. 221)

Ten percent of the households receiving Aid to Families with Dependent Children are headed by men. Ninety percent of the households are headed by women.
(Bird, p. 32)

Air Force Academy Cadets
11.4 percent of Air Force Academy cadets are female.
(Hacker, p. 207)

Air Force Enlisted Personnel
11.3 percent of enlisted Air Force personnel are female.
(Hacker, p. 207)

Air Force Officers
8.7 percent of all Air Force officers are female.
(*Hacker, p. 207*)

Alcohol and Drug Addiction
Male: Fifteen percent of alcoholic men are also addicted to other drugs.
Female: Twenty-nine percent of alcoholic women are addicted to other drugs.
(*From a nationwide survey by Alcoholics Anonymous; Levy, p. 196*)

Alcoholics Anonymous
One in three people who joined A.A. between 1977 and 1980 were female. (Two out of three women utilize alcohol.)
(*1981 Gallup Poll; Redbook, June 1982; p. 77*)

Alcoholism
Male: Approximately 7.3 percent of all men are alcoholics. Between two thirds and five sixths of all alcoholics are male. There are 7 to 14 million male alcholics in the United States.
Female: Three percent of all women are alcoholics. Between one sixth and one third of all alcoholics are women. There are three to six million female alcoholics in the United States. Two out of three women being treated for alcoholism are under thirty-five.
(*Woman's Body, p. 333*)

Alcoholism, Treatment Grants for
Only 3 percent of the treatment grants given by the National Institute on Alcohol Abuse and Alcoholism are for the treatment of women. The other 97 percent go toward treatment for men.
(*Bird, p. 127*)

Alcoholism and Marital Stability
Male: One out of every ten husbands stay with alcoholic wives.
Female: Nine out of every ten wives stay with alcoholic husbands.
(*Lake, p. 78*)

Alcohol Reaction
Male: Excess alcohol consumption can cause reduced testoster-

one levels, which may lead to lessened sexual activity and/or temporary impotence.

Female: Women are affected by alcoholic beverages more rapidly than men as they do not have as much water in their bodies to dilute the alcohol as do men. Excess alcohol cannot only decrease the intensity of orgasm, but can make orgasm difficult to achieve.

(*Hoffman, pp. 68–72;* Health and Longevity Report, *Vol. 2, No. 2, p. 5*)

Alone, Living

The following is a breakdown, by age group, of the percentages of males and females who live alone:

Male:
15–24—12.4%

25–44—44%

45–64—23.6%

Female:
15–24—6.4%

25–44—16.7%

45–64—25.2%

20 percent of those living alone are males over age sixty-five.
51.6 percent of those living alone are females over sixty-five.

(Almanac, *1983, p. 784*)

Altruism

There are no known sex differences, although some feel women are the more altruistic.

(*Ford, p. 112*)

Alzheimer's Disease

Equal numbers of men and women are victims of Alzheimer's disease, a disorder that destroys certain vital cells in the brain, resulting in intellectual impairment for 2 to 4 million Americans.

(Kako'o, *Alzheimer's Disease*)

Amphetamines Prescribed by a Physician

Males: Five million men have utilized amphetamines ordered by a doctor.

Females: Twelve million women have taken amphetamines on doctors' orders.

(*Levy, p. 196*)

Amyotrophic Lateral Sclerosis (Lou Gehrig's Disease)

(ALS is a disease characterized by progressive weakness and wasting of the skeletal muscles. The cause is unknown, but it may be related to genetics, mercury poisoning, or other causes. The disease is fatal, with a life expectancy of two to five years.)
ALS is more common in men than women, on a 1.5 to 1 ratio.
(Ha'ilono Kina, *November 1981, cover page*)

Analgesics

Women take 76 percent of the analgesics prescribed.
(Bird, p. 126)

Analogies

Females excel in analogies.
(*Wagenvoord/Bailey*, Women, p. 24)

Analytic Reasoning

Boys of age twelve and under are better than girls of the same age at analytic reasoning. Some authorities attribute this to the "hands-on" method utilized by teachers who give special individualized instruction to boys more frequently than to girls.
(Serbin and O'Leary, p. 102)

Androgens

Androgens are primarily male hormones but are also found in varying amounts in females. The most prominent androgen, testosterone, is ten to fifteen times higher in the male than in the female. Androgens increase in the female after menopause, and a woman's voice may deepen and facial hair may increase.
(Money, p. 206)

Androgynous Behaviors

(The androgynous person is one whose behavior is determined by what is appropriate and effective rather than by what is stereotypically masculine and/or feminine.)
In a study of child care workers and male engineers, the following behaviors of the adults toward the children were noted:
Males: Both male and female workers and engineers endorsed masculine stereotyped behaviors and traits for boys, i.e., that they should be tough, courageous, aggressive, and independent.

Females: All of the child care workers and the engineers endorsed androgynous behaviors for the girls—i.e., aggressive, independent, etc., as well as "soft"; that it was okay to be gentle, giving, sensitive.

(*Robinson, Skeen, Flake-Hobson, p. 240*)

Androsterone

Androsterone is a scent given off by men when perspiring, thought to arouse sexual desire in females. Wild bears and pigs also emit this odor, which prompts aggression in the males and a receptivity to mating in sows.

There have been several inconclusive experiments concerned with the question of whether females are sexually aroused by this odor. However, some tests have indicated that young ovulating females are particularly sensitive to it.

(*White, pp. 9–12*)

Anemia, Pernicious

Pernicious anemia is one of several diseases that are more often fatal to women than to men. The disease is associated with a lack of hydrochloric acid in the body. This interferes with the body's ability to absorb vitamin B_{12}, which in turn leads to a reduction of red blood cells. Symptoms include paleness, numbness, loss of appetite, nausea, and diarrhea. Other diseases in which the mortality rate of women leads that of men are diabetes, uterine and breast cancer, and abnormalities of childbirth.

(*Cooke and Dworkin, p. 405*)

Annapolis Cadets

6.65 percent of the cadets who attend Annapolis are female.

(*Hacker, p. 207*)

Anorexia Nervosa

(A psychiatric disorder involving a compulsive drive for thinness, leading to a disgust for food.)

This is seen more commonly in females, affecting approximately one of every two hundred women. Less than 7 percent of anorexics are male. Mortality is high at 5 to 15 percent.

(*Knickerbocker, p. 130; Kolb, p. 66*)

Antibodies

"Women are better at producing antibodies" than are men, and thus "have a lower incidence of viral and bacterial diseases." The reason is that males have only one X chromosome, whereas women have two. The X chromosome carries some of the genes that control immunity. Thus, if something goes wrong with the first, the second can take over. A man has only one X chromosome (and one Y, which determines the male sex, and contains the programming for the production of male hormones and masculine development).

(Science Digest, *September 1982, p. 90; Hammer, p. 22*)

Antidepressant

Seventy-six percent of the antidepressants prescribed are for use by women.

(*Frankfort and Burtle, p. 96*)

Anxiety and Close Proximity

Male: Men display less anxiety if there is space between them and other people.
Female: Women usually find support in being able to touch one another.

(*Researchers: Gregory Nicasia and John R. Aielo, Rutgers University;* Human Behavior, *March 1978, p. 27*)

Anxiety Test

In tests, women display higher levels of anxiety than men.

(*Dowling, p. 49*)

Aphasia

(Difficulty speaking properly due to brain damage.)
Males are affected more often than females.

(*Arkoff, p. 64*)

Appetite for Food

The appetites of males and females for food are identical.

(*Edelstein, p. 14*)

Architects
93.3 percent of architects are male.
(*Goleman, p. 59; Hacker, p. 128*)

Armed Forces Commissioned Officers, Numbers of
Males: There are 76,237 male commissioned officers.
Females: There are 6,880 women commissioned officers.
(Almanac, *1981, p. 311*)

Armed Forces Disciplinary Problems
There are more disciplinary problems with males than with females.
(*Adams, p. 53*; Psychology Today, *October 1980*)

Armed Forces Enlisted Personnel
Males: There are 608,223 enlisted men in the U.S. armed forces.
Females: There are 58,203 enlisted women in the armed forces.
(Almanac, *l981, p. 311*)

Arms
The male arm forms one even line from the shoulder to the wrist, whereas the female arm angles out from her body.
(*Wagenvoord/Bailey*, Women, *p. 64*)

Army Enlisted Personnel
9.1 percent of army enlisted personnel are female.
(*Hacker, p. 207*)

Army Generals
Male: There are four hundred ten male army generals.
Female: There are two female army generals.
(*Field, p. 78*)

Army Volunteers Who Fail to Finish the First Year of Enlistment
Male: 33.2 percent resign before completing the first year of service.
Female: 46.7 percent resign before the end of the first year of service.
(*Adams, p. 50*; Psychology Today, *October 1980*)

Arousal, Sexual
Men are more quickly aroused than women.
   (Brothers, p. 142)

Arrests, Total for 1980
Male: 7,982,339 men were arrested in 1980.
Female: 1,501,619 women were arrested in 1980.
   (Almanac, 1983, p. 783)

Arrests for Drunkenness
Males: 914,000 men were arrested for drunkenness in 1980.
Females: 75,800 women were arrested for drunkenness in 1980.
   (Census, 1980, p. 180)

Arrests for Serious Crimes
Males: 1,682,000 men were arrested for serious crimes in 1980.
Females: 392,000 women were arrested for serious crimes in 1980.
   (Census, 1980, p. 180)

Art, Recognition and Acclaim
Ninety percent of the masterpieces at the Metropolitan Museum in New York were done by men.
   (Bird, p. 87)

Art History, Faculty Positions
Male: Seventy-five percent of art history professors are men.
Female: Twenty-five percent of art history professors are women.
   (Bird, p. 88)

Art History, Graduate Degrees in
The same number of men and women obtain art history degrees.
   (Bird, p. 88)

Art Students
Male: Twenty-five percent of art students are male.
Female: Seventy-five percent of art students are female.
   (Bird, p. 88)

Arterial Hypertension
Arterial hypertension is defined as over:
    130/90 for men under age forty-five
    145/95 for men over forty-five
    160/95 for women
The risks related to arterial hypertension are greater for males (especially blacks).
    (Eiseman, p. 50)

Arteriosclerosis
Men are more likely to have arteriosclerosis than women.
    (Brothers, Woman's Day, 2/9/82; p. 138)

Arthritis and Age
Males: After age sixty, many men develop degenerative arthritis. *Females:* Beginning at age thirty or so, women may develop rheumatoid arthritis. Women are twice as likely to suffer from arthritis as men are.
    (Man's Body, pp. C01–04)

Aspirin Users (over 20 Years of Age)
Male: 39.6 million men use aspirin.
Female: 54.6 million women use aspirin.
    (U.S. Statistical Abstract, 1982, p. 123)

Assembly Lines
More women than men work on assembly lines.
    (Murphy, p. 50)

Assertive Interactions
Men are more effective in assertive interactions than are women. Many feel this is due to the differences in the training of the sexes. Women have traditionally been taught to be dependent, submissive, and to "go along," whereas men have been expected to be assertive. (One can easily understand the popularity of female assertiveness training classes.)
    (Franks and Burtle, pp. 298–99)

Assistance, Energy
Eighty-five percent of the homes that are eligible for energy as-

sistance for low-income households are headed by women.
(*Ehrenreich and Stallard, p. 221*)

Asthma, Bronchial
Men are more susceptible to bronchial asthma than women are.
(*Brothers*, Woman's Day, 2/9/82, p. 138)

Astronauts
Ten percent of the American astronauts are female.
(U.S. News & World Report, 11/29/82, p. 54)

Athletes, High School
In 1983, for every one hundred male athletes in high school, there were thirty-six female athletes. This is in contrast to the 1972 figures of eighteen female for every hundred male high school athletes.
(*Caudle, p. 8*)

Athletes, Subcutaneous Fat
Male: Some men have as little as 4 to 6 percent "under the skin" fat.
Female: Women athletes usually have about 10 to 15 percent subcutaneous fat, but their levels can go as low as those of men.
(*Klafs and Arnheim, p. 184*)

Athletics, in Pool and Track
Men are about 10 percent faster on the track and in the pool than women.
(*Gelman, p. 75*)

Attorneys
90.6 percent of attorneys are male.
(*Department of Labor, 1979*)

Attraction
Males: Attraction can be purely physical.
Females: Women are attracted to wealth and position or skill.
(*Wilder, p. 105*)

Attraction and Appearance

Male: In a survey reported by *Ms.* magazine, physical appearance was listed first by men and boys as the trait they most desired in a partner. In a survey reported by *Psychology Today*, the three things men notice first in a woman are her figure, her face, and how she is dressed.

Female: In the same survey by *Ms.*, a man's appearance was rarely at the top of the list of traits women desired in men. In the survey reported by *Psychology Today*, females tended to notice how he is dressed, his eyes and figure.

(*Ms.*, 2/83; Hunt, p. 17; Survey by the Roper Organization)

Attractiveness and Fun

Good-looking men have more fun than good-looking women.

(Jones, p. 1, Section C)

Attention-Getting Behaviors by Children

Males: Boys utilize aggressive and disruptive behavior as a means of getting attention in school.

Females: Girls utilize withdrawn and dependent behaviors as methods of getting attention.

(Serbin and O'Leary, p. 57)

Average Male and Female—Measurements

Males: The average male is five feet nine inches tall, and weighs 162 pounds. His chest measures thirty-eight and three quarters inches; his waist is thirty-one and three quarters inches.

(Man's Body, pp. A19–21)

Females: The average woman is five feet three inches tall and weighs 135 pounds. Her bust is thirty-five and one half inches; her waist is twenty-nine and one quarter inches; and her hips are thirty-eight inches.

(Woman's Body, p. 18)

Aviation Hall of Fame

Males: There are eighty men in the Aviation Hall of Fame.

Females: There are four women in the Aviation Hall of Fame.

(Almanac, 1981, p. 213)

Auditory Comprehension
Women exceed men in auditory comprehension.
(Goleman, p. 49)

Auditory Memory
Men are inferior to women in auditory memory.
(Newsweek, 5/18/81; p. 73)

Autistic
There are 2.75 autistic males to every 1 autistic female.
(Kolb, p. 340)

Autoimmune Diseases
Women's immunity systems are so efficient that they sometimes attack their own tissues, resulting in diseases such as lupus (inflammation of the connective tissue), rheumatoid arthritis, and myasthenia gravis (muscular disease). All of these disorders are more frequent in women than men.
(Science Digest, September 1982, p. 90)

Auto Mechanics
In 1980, 99.3 percent of auto mechanics were male.
(Hacker, p. 127)

B

Bachelor Degrees Awarded in the 1979–80 Academic Year
Male: Males earn 50.8 percent of all bachelor degrees.
Female: Women earn 49.2 percent of all bachelor degrees.
(*Hacker, p. 242*)

Bacterial Infections
Women are more immune than men to bacterial infections.
(Science Digest, 9/82, p. 90)

Ball Sports
Men do better than women in ball sports, as males' arms are longer and composed of more muscle fiber. Both characteristics aid them in throwing and hitting.
(*Wagenvoord/Bailey*, Men, p. 61)

Bank Tellers
In 1980 92.7 percent of the bank tellers were female.
(*Hacker, p. 128*)

Barr Bodies
A Barr body is a small dot in the central living part of a cell (the nucleus of a cell that contains the chromosomes), which stains easily when prepared for microscopic examination. It is absent in males but present in females. Some alleged female athletes were disqualified from the Olympic Games over ten years ago

due to an absence of Barr bodies in the cells scraped from the mucous membrane lining inside the cheek.
    (*Rothenberg, p. 33, 50, 216; Wagenvoord/Bailey* Men, *p. 18*)

Basal Metabolic Rate

Males: Adult males utilize an average of 39.5 calories per square meter of body surface every hour. This lowers to 36.5 at age sixty. (Boys twelve years old burn 50 calories per square meter!) *Females:* Females burn approximately 37 calories per square meter of body surface per hour. This is reduced to 34 at age sixty.
    (*Cooke and Dworkin, p. 53*)

Bathing Suits

Males: Two out of five men told interviewers that they feel the current bathing suits are too revealing.
Females: Three out of five women told interviewers that the suits younger women are wearing these days are too revealing.
    (*Lou Boyd*)

Battered Children

Records show that men batter children more than women do.
    (National Analysis of Official Child Abuse and Neglect Reporting,
    1977; *p. 42*)

Battered Husbands and Wives

Males: 282,000 men are beaten by their wives annually. Women are most likely to throw things, bite, hit with the fist, or threaten with a gun or knife.
Females: Six million wives are abused yearly in this country, with two thousand to four thousand being beaten to death by their husbands or lovers. Battery is the single major cause of injury to women. Men are more likely to push, shove, beat the woman up, and use a gun or knife.
    (*O'Reilly, p. 23;* Human Behavior, *November 1978, p. 80*)

Batting

Males: excel at batting balls due to stronger and broader shoulders. A man's bones are longer, giving him greater leverage, which, combined with greater strength, enables him to hit a ball harder than a woman.

    (Selden, p. 53)

Bedwetting
Bedwetting occurs more frequently among males than among females.

    (Simonds and Parraga, p. 386)

Behavioral Differences at Two Months of Age
Males: Boys are particularly attracted to visual stimuli—a tendency that seems to persist throughout life. Boys eat more, and are more curious and more active than girls.

Females: Girls respond more to auditory stimuli. This also persists throughout life. Girl babies cry more than boy babies, eat less, and are less active.

    (Gottlieb, p. 80)

Billfolds, Color Preference for
Males prefer black billfolds. Females prefer brown.

    (Boyd, Honolulu Advertiser, 7/1/82)

Billing Clerks
90.2 percent of all billing clerks are female.

    (Hacker, p. 128)

Birth Control, Most Popular Method for
For American couples married one year or more, sterilization is the most popular birth control method. Of those married at least one year, 8 million men and women have been sterilized.

    (Woman's Body, pp. 74–76)

Birth Control Measures
Males: Men have the option to use the Bionex control method, in which a clasp-shaped device in the form of a T is fitted inside the sperm duct and can be turned off and on, depending on whether or not contraception is desired, as well as the condom, the new male pill, or vasectomy.

Females: Women can utilize the pill (see *Pill*), the rhythm

method, the I.U.D., the diaphragm, foam, abortion, or sterilization, which usually involves "tying the tubes."
(*Cooke/Dworkin, pp. 36–91*)

Birth Control Responsibility
Males: It is the opinion of most men that birth control is the
female's responsibility.
Females: Females also feel it is the responsibility of the woman.
(*Peplau, Rubin, and Hill, p. 142*)

Birth Defects
In one study, of 190 birth defects observed, 71 percent of the
infants affected were male.
(*Dranov, p. 32*)

Birth Injuries
Males are more likely to suffer from birth injuries than are
females.
(*Arkoff, p. 66*)

Birth Ratios
There are 106 males born to every 100 females.
(Man's Body, *pp. A01–02*)

Birth Weight, Average Differences of
Males: The average boy weighs seven and a half pounds at birth.
Females: The average girl weighs seven pounds at birth.
(Man's Body, *p. A05- 06*)

Births
Males: 1,709,394 males were born in 1978.
Females: 1,623,885 females were born in 1978. There were 5 per-
cent more male births than female.
(Almanac, *1980, p. 137*)
Males: 1,791,267 males were born in 1979.
Females: 1,703,131 females were born in 1979.
(Almanac, *1983, p. 791*)
For every 1,000 females, 1,052 boys are born each year.
(*Hacker, p. 53*)

Blood, Amount of
Males: Men have about one gallon of blood.
Females: Women have approximately four fifths of a gallon of blood.
(*Wagenvoord/Bailey*, Men, p. 68)

Blood, Number of Red Corpuscles
"Men have about 20 percent more red blood corpuscles than women."
(*Brothers*, Woman's Day, 2/19/82, p. 138)

Blood Cells
Men have an average of 1 million more blood cells in every drop of blood than women do.
(*Wagenvoord/Bailey*, Men, p. 68)

Blood Clotting
A man's blood clots faster than a woman's and is thicker.
(*Foley*, p. 59)

Blood Manufacture
Men manufacture blood less effectively than women do, as the female's cardiovascular system is, as a whole, superior to the male's.
(*Brothers*, Woman's Day, 2/19/82, p. 138 and 139; Marvit, M.D. [interview])

Blood Pressure, Average Reading of
Males: The average blood pressure for a male is 140/88.
Females: The average reading for a female is 130/80.
(*Murray*, p. 60)

Blood Pressure and Hormones
Male: The male hormone testosterone seems to increase the likelihood of high blood pressure.
Female: After menopause, women lose the balance of hormones that some authorities feel gives them protection against high blood pressure. Thus high blood pressure is a problem for many older women.
(*Brothers*, Woman's Day, 2/9/82, p. 138; Dustan, pages unnumbered)

Blood Vessels and Color Differences
The blood vessels of men are redder than those of women.
(Brothers, p. 5)

Blood, Weight of
A man's blood is heavier than a woman's.
(Brothers, Woman's Day, 2/9/82, p. 138)

Bloody Urine and Jogging
Male: Some men pass bloody urine after jogging. This is a result of repeated impact of the empty bladder against the prostate. Some physicians advise men not to empty their bladders completely prior to running.
Women: Symptoms of this nature have not been reported.
(Healthwise, sample issue, 1982, p. 1)

"Blue' Balls"
Males: This is the name describing discomfort due to lack of orgasm following sexual excitement among males.
Females: If orgasm does not occur in women, and high levels of sexual excitement result in pelvic congestion that leads to pain, discomfort, and physical complications, it is called Taylors Syndrome.
(Starr, p. 68)

Blue-Collar Workers, Skilled
Of the approximately 11 million skilled blue-collar workers in 1976, only 545,038 were women.
(Bird, p. 117)

Bluffers
Males: Men are said to "bluff it" when they are unsure of their ground.
Females: A woman does not usually "bluff." If she feels she is right, a woman will stand her ground even more strongly than a man will.
(Eppingham, p. 37)

Body Temperature
The average temperature of a man is slightly higher than that of a woman. It peaks at midday in both sexes.
(*Selden, p. 52*)

Bone Loss
("A loss in the bony substances resulting in brittleness and softness of bones."
[*Rothenberg, p. 22*])
Male: Bone loss occurs in males but is much less of a problem than it is in women.
Female: After age forty-five, women begin to lose bone density at a rate of about 1 percent per year. Loss of bone mass, and increased bone porosity and thickness, make women more susceptible to breaks, strains, and various bone diseases.
(*Cooley, p. 459*)

Bones
The bones of a man are stronger, heavier, and larger than those of a woman. His shoulders are also broader and his pelvic bone is narrower.
(*Brothers, Woman's Day, 2/9/82; p. 138*)

Bookkeepers
90.5 percent of bookkeepers are female.
(*Hacker, p. 128*)

Brain, Biochemical Differences in
Women's brains are more sensitive to experimentally administered lights and sounds than men's are. (It is speculated that this is the result of the action of a certain hormone in the formation of key brain chemicals.)
(*Buchsbaum, p. 96*)

Brain, Blood Supply to
Women have a better blood supply to the brain than men do, because of a more effective cardiovascular system.
(*Irving Marvit, M.D. [interview]*)

Brain, Differences in Organization of

Male: The way in which the male brain is organized may orient a man toward visual-spacial superiority. His brain is specialized, receiving spatial problems in the right side of the brain and verbal problems in the left side of the brain.

Female: Women are believed to be more left-side oriented and are able to handle verbal material more effectively than men. The female brain is not specialized, but duplicates abilities on both sides. Both sides of the brain work together on a problem. The female brain is more generalized. Some people feel this is why women are able to make faster decisions than men and are more perceptive. In addition, if one side of a woman's brain is damaged by stroke, the other side, which duplicates the abilities of the damaged side, can take over, and the woman can hopefully regain her abilities. This is not true in men. If a man has a stroke and the left side of his brain is damaged, he may lose his ability to speak because the right side of his brain handles only spatial problems.

    (Foley, p. 59; Newsweek, 5/18/81, p. 81; Brothers, pp. 32, 33; Hammer, p. 25)

Brain Damage

Women have a much lower risk of brain damage due to tumors and strokes than men do.

    (Goleman, p. 51)

Brain Differences in Children

Boys: The right side (spatial side) develops earlier in boys than it does in girls.

Girls: The left side (verbal side) develops earlier in females.

    (Wagenvoord/Bailey, Men, p. 27; Science Digest, 3/82, p. 99)

Brain-Injured at Birth

More males than females are brain-injured at birth.

    (Arkoff, p. 64)

Brain Size

The brain of a male is 14 percent larger than that of a female.

    (Newsweek, 5/18/81, p. 81)

Breaks, Coffee
Males: Males spend an average of fifty-two minutes a day on coffee breaks.
Females: Females spend about thirty-five minutes a day on coffee breaks.
(*Researcher: University of Michigan Institute of Social Research; Fogg, p. 18*)

Breast Enlargement and Valium
Males: Breast enlargement has been reported in men due to taking Valium. (It is felt that this is because Valium converts the male hormone into a female hormone in the tissues.)
Females: There are no reports of breast enlargement due to taking Valium.
(Healthwise, Vol. 5, No. 1)

Breathing
Male: Men tend to breathe from the diaphragm, to breathe deeper than women, and less often. They take an average of sixteen breaths per minute, or 17,300 breaths daily.
Female: Women breathe more often, from the upper part of the chest, and their breathing is more shallow than that of men. They take an average of approximately twenty to twenty-two breaths per minute, or 28,800 breaths daily. Both sexes inhale about 2,300 gallons of air per day.
(*Klafs and Arnheim, p. 183; Boyd, 7/1/82, p. 24;* Science Digest, *7/82, p. 96*)

Bronchitis
Men are more likely to have bronchitis than women are.
(*Brothers,* Woman's Day, *2/9/82, p. 138*)

Brucellosis
(Undulant fever acquired from animals or animal products)
Men are more vulnerable to brucellosis than women are. This disease is characterized by sudden onset of fever and great weakness.
(*Grollman, p. 749*)

Bulimia
(Bulimia is an eating disorder in which a person first goes on an eating binge and then induces vomiting. It is said that the latter

is an attempt to gain control of eating. Thirty percent of college girls are said to practice the binge-purge behavior.)
Male: 5 percent of those afflicted with bulimia are male.
Female: 95 percent of those afflicted with bulimia are female.
(Newsweek, *11/2/81, p. 60*)

Buoyancy
Women are more buoyant in the water, due to higher levels of body fat, than men. Fat floats!
(Newsweek, *5/18/81, p. 75*)

Bus Drivers
50 percent of bus drivers are male.
(*Murphy, p. 51*)

Business, Average Income for
Male: In 1979 the average income for men who owned their own businesses amounted to $41,558.
Female: In 1979, the average income for women who owned their own businesses amounted to $12,826.
(*Hacker, p. 137*)

Business, Awarding of Federal Contracts
Less than 1 percent of more than $130 billion in government contracts were awarded to businesses owned by women. The rest of the contracts went to male-owned businesses.
(*Bird, p. 98*)

Business Management and Administration
Male: 351 doctorates in business management and administration were awarded to men in 1980.
Female: 59 were awarded to women.
(U.S. Statistical Abstract, *p. 166*)

Business Management and Administration
Male: 23,559 master's degrees in business management and administration were awarded to men in 1980.
Female: 6,199 were awarded to women.
(U.S. Statistical Abstract, *p. 166*)

Cabinetmakers
96.3 percent of cabinetmakers are male.

(Hacker, p. 128)

Calcium Metabolic Rate
The female metabolizes calcium faster than the male, as ossification (hardening) of her bones occurs earlier. The bones of the male are harder and more dense than those of the female because of the slower rate of hardening, and the consequent calcium retention.

(Klafs and Arnheim, p. 184)

Caloric Needs (Estimate)
Males: Men can multiply their body weight fifteen times to figure their basic daily caloric need. Add about 700 calories for extra energy during the day.

(You and Your Heart, p. 9)

Females: Women can multiply their weight ten times to determine the number of calories needed to "run" the body and maintain basic life functions such as breathing, the beating of the heart, and digestion. Add about 500 extra calories for extra energy needed.

(Edelstein, p. 12)

Calories, Average Consumed
Males: Men consume about 2,700 calories a day.

Females: Women consume about 2,000 calories a day.
(Family Circle, *September 1975, p. 130*)

Calories Burned
Women have a lower metabolic rate (the rate at which calories
are burned for energy) and burn only ten to fifteen calories per
pound of body weight, whereas men burn seventeen to twenty
calories per pound of body weight, even when engaging in the
same activity.
(*Edelstein, p. 12*)

Calories Utilized per Hour, While Sedentary
Male: Men utilize 3.7 calories per hour for each square foot of
skin surface.
Female: Women burn only 3.5 calories per hour per square foot
of skin surface.
(*Brothers, Woman's Day, 2/9/82, p. 138*)

Cancer
Cancer occurs more often in men than in women.
(Woman's Body, *p. B38*)

Cancer, Colon
Colon cancer occurs more often in men, but is the third leading
cause of cancer-related deaths for both sexes.
(*Eiseman, p. 48*)

Cancer, Cure Rate
Males: The cure rate for men is lower than that for women. Many
believe that is due to the fact that they have fewer physical
exams and smoke more than women, and that they have an inferior immune system.
Females: Women have a better cure rate than men. Many feel it
is because they have more frequent physical exams so that early
diagnosis is more likely, but the most likely reason is that the
female is physically healthier than the male and has a superior
immune system.
(What Everyone Should Know About Cancer, *p. 8*)

Cancer, Digestive
Males: Cancer of the digestive system accounts for 27 percent of the cancer deaths in men.
Females: Digestive system cancer accounts for 29 percent of the cancer deaths in women.
(What Everyone Should Know About Cancer, *p. 9*)

Cancer, Fatalities
Males: Fifty-five percent of all cancer deaths are men.
Females: Forty-five percent of all cancer deaths are women.
(What Everyone Should Know About Cancer, *p. 9*)

Cancer, Lung
Over the past thirty years, the incidence of lung cancer has increased 300 percent among women and 175 percent in men.
Males: Lung cancer kills 50,000 men annually, and accounts for 33 percent of all cancer deaths.
Females: Lung cancer kills 10,000 women annually, and accounts for 11 percent of all cancer deaths in women.
(What Everyone Should Know About Cancer, *p. 9*)

Cancer, Lymphoma and Leukemia
More men than women contract lymphoma and leukemia.
(*Brothers,* Woman's Day, *2/9/82, p. 138*)

Cancer, Most Fatal in Both Sexes
Males: Cancer of the lung is the most fatal cancer for men.
Females: Cancer of the breast is the most fatal cancer for women.
(*Eiseman, p. 48*)

Cancer, Sites of
Male: skin—23% of all cancers
            lung—18%
            colon/rectal—11%
            digestive—13%
            leukemia—7%
            prostate—13%
            urinary—6%
            other—9%

Female: skin—13%
            lung—5%
            colon/rectal—13%
            digestive—7%
            leukemia—6%
            breast—23%
            uterus—14%
            other—19%
    (Man's Body, *pp. B35–37*)

Cancer and Diet
Males: Sixty percent of cancers in men can be attributed to improper diet.
Females: Forty-one percent of cancers in women can be attributed to improper diet.
    (Nutrition News, *1981, Vol. IV, No. 8*)

Cancer and Smoking
Smoking is responsible for 83 percent of lung cancers among men, and 43 percent among women.
    (*Eiseman, p. 67*)

Cancer Mortality and Sexual Differences
In all countries except Iceland, cancer kills more men than women.
    (Man's Body, *pp. B33–34*)

Candidiasis (Also known as thrush)
Males: Men can be carriers of candidiasis, but seldom have symptoms.
Females: About 20 percent of women have candidiasis. However, the disease causes symptoms in only about one out of a hundred. The symptoms appear as a white discharge and itching in the area of the vagina and vulva.
    (Man's Body, *p. M25*)

Captains in the Armed Services
Of 85,778 captains in the armed services, 7,681 are women.
    (*Hacker, p. 206*)

Carbohydrate Intolerance
Overweight women have difficulty metabolizing carbohydrates, and tend to convert them to fat rather than to energy as males do.
(Edelstein, p. 101)

Carbohydrate-Rich Foods, Craving for
More women than men have seemingly uncontrollable cravings for carbohydrate-rich foods. Some scientists feel this is due to the activity of a brain chemical called serotonin, which may help to regulate cravings for such foods. The activity of this chemical normally increases after the consumption of even a few calories, and desire decreases accordingly. However, in some overweight women (and some men), the activity does not increase, and the desire for more rich food does not decrease as it does normally.
(Chestnutt, pp. 60 and 62)

Carbon Dioxide Output
Boys may exhale as much as 40 percent more carbon dioxide than girls do.
(Sexton, p. 74)

Cardiovascular Differences
Women have smaller hearts, less total blood volume, smaller amounts of total hemoglobin (which carries oxygen to the muscles), and a lower oxygen pulse (the oxygen one can process per heartbeat) than men.
(Brothers, Woman's Day, 2/9/82, p. 138; Irving Marvit, M.D., interview)

Carpenters
98.5 percent of carpenters are male.
(Hacker, p. 127)

Carpet Installers
98.7 percent of carpet installers are male.
(Hacker, p. 127)

Carrying Angle
The angle formed in the crook of the elbow when the arm is held akimbo is six degrees greater in a woman than in a man. It is felt

by most that the wider angle (combined with the added width of
the woman's hips) facilitates carrying a child.

(*Wagenvoord/Bailey*, Women, *p. 64*)

Cellulite

(Cellulite is the deposit of fat on a woman's legs and buttocks
that will not "go away" with either exercise or diet. There are
several theories on the causes of cellulite, among them that it is a
mixture of fat, water, and toxins that should be eliminated by the
body but are not. Some attribute the waffled appearance of the
fat to fat cells, explaining that some cells retain enormous
amounts of fat in certain parts of the body and that in women
this occurs around the hips or legs.)

Males: Men do not have cellulite.

Females: Eight out of ten women have cellulite.

(*Health, Education and Human Services Publication No. 80, p. 1078*)

Center of Gravity

The female has a lower center of gravity than the male, due to
differences in shoulder and hip widths. Women have narrower
shoulders and wider hips.

(*Selden, p. 53*)

Chambermaids

97 percent of chambermaids are female.

(*Hacker, p. 127*)

Change of Life

Males: There is no sudden, obvious sign indicating a change of
life (as with the female's cessation of menses); rather, a decrease
of testosterone occurs gradually. The depression that some men
feel at middle age, when they realize they will not be able to
achieve what they expected, is often called male menopause. It
usually occurs between the ages of thirty-five and fifty.

Females: Menopause is a process characterized by a cessation of
menses, at which point a woman becomes infertile. It is felt that
the reduction of estrogen and the cessation of progesterone production is responsible for the uncomfortable physical symptoms
such as hot flashes, and the psychological symptoms such as de-

pression, that some climacteric women report. Menopause usually occurs between ages forty-five and fifty-five.

(Woman's Body, *pp. 181–195*)

Change of Life Symptoms, Physical
Males: No symptoms have been reported.
Females: The physical symptoms often include hot flashes, sleeplessness, irritability, weight gain, dizzy spells, palpitations, night sweats, and vaginal dryness.

(Woman's Body, *pp. 181–195*)

Change of Life Symptoms, Psychological
Males: Many men fear they will not attain their goals or "make their mark" when they begin to be aware they are at middle age. They report depression, and an anxiety about death, health, and marriage is not uncommon.
Females: Many women become depressed at menopause due to both physical and emotional stress. They may fear loss of attractiveness or of their role in society, an inability to find employment due to age, and the loss of fertility.

(Cooke/Dworkin, *p. 317*)

Checks, Writing of
In two thirds of the households contacted, it was the woman who wrote the checks and paid the bills, whether she worked outside the home or not.

(Friermuth, *p. 13*)

Child Abuse, Perpetrators of
Males: An estimated 11,960 males abused children in 1977.
Females: Some 9,389 females abused children in 1977.

(National Analysis of Official Child Abuse and Neglect Reporting,
1977, p. 42)

Child Care
Men and women share this function, but women tend to resist sharing child care in spite of the fact that men enjoy fathering.

(Pogrebin, *p. 144*)

Child Care Providers
97.4 percent of child-care workers are female.
(Hacker, p. 127)

Child Neglect, Perpetrators of
(The legal definition of child neglect differs from state to state, but in general it can be viewed as [1] physical neglect of one's child, which can include inadequate diet, lack of medical care, sexual or physical abuse; [2] emotional neglect, which includes rejection, and denial of normal experiences that produce feelings of being loved and wanted; [3] material neglect, which includes insufficient clothes, food, or shelter; [4] demoralizing circumstances such as continual friction in the home, mentally ill parents, excessive drinking or drug abuse, or encouragement of delinquent behaviors.

[Child Abuse and Neglect, *p. 21*])
Males: 13,905 males legally neglected children in 1977.
Females: 28,007 females legally neglected children in 1977.
(National Analysis of Official Child Abuse and Neglect Reporting, *1977*)

Chlamydia
(Chlamydia is the most common venereal disease in the United States. It is estimated that 4 million Americans are stricken by it each year.)
Males: Men who have contracted the disease often have pain, discharge, and burning.
Females: Women often display no symptoms.
(*Mind and Body*, Science Digest, *May 1982, p. 99*)

Choice of Person to Accomplish a Challenging Task
When confronted with the task of assigning an important job, both male and female business people tend to choose a member of their own sex.
(Cory, Psychology Today, *October 1982, p. 22*)

Chromosomes, Numbers of
In human beings, the female ovum and the male sperm each possess 23 chromosomes. Thus, each person has a total of 46.
Males: Men have one X chromosome and one Y chromosome in every cell.

Females: Women have two X chromosomes in every cell. They can get their X's from either parent.

(*Bishop, p. 1*)

Churchgoers

More women than men are churchgoers.

(*Eppingham, p. 37*)

Cirrhosis of the Liver

Women who drink heavily are twice as likely to develop cirrhosis of the liver than are men. The cirrhosis also develops at an earlier age and after a briefer period of excessive drinking.

(*National Council on Alcoholism*)

Clergy

95.8 percent of the clergy are male.

(*Hacker, p. 128*)

Clerical, Service, and Sales Jobs

Males: Twenty percent of the males in the work force are employed in clerical, service, and sales jobs.

Females: Sixty percent of the women in the work force are employed in clerical, service, and sales jobs.

(*Newsline*, Psychology Today, *December, 1981, p. 19*)

Climbing

Men are better climbers than women because the manner in which the woman's thigh is joined to her knees makes climbing more awkward for her.

(*Brothers,* Woman's Day, *2/9/83, p. 138*)

Coaches

In the years 1975 to 1980, the number of coaches and assistant coaches for women's sports increased 37 percent at the University of California, but the majority of coaches were men, not women. The number of female coaches increased only 3 percent, and the number of female head coaches dropped 20 percent. Researchers found that athletic directors tended to hire men, as they felt men could produce winning teams by using more discipline, because they have more experience, and because they are more organized than female coaches, whom they perceive as serving as role models, and knowing more about the rules of women's sports.

(*Cory*, Psychology Today, *May 1980, p. 20*)

Coffee Drinkers

Male: 46.1 million men in the U.S.A. are coffee drinkers.
Female: 54.9 million women in the U.S.A. are coffee drinkers.

(U.S. Statistical Abstract, *p. 123*)

Cold

Men are more sensitive to cold than women are, as females have a layer of fat under the skin that provides additional warmth.

(*Klafs and Arnheim, p. 184*)

College Degrees

Male: In the academic year 1979–80, 50.8 percent of all college degrees were awarded to men.
Female: 49.2 percent were awarded to women.

(*Hacker, p. 242*)

College Faculty

Although the majority of college students are female, the majority of professors are male.

(Time, *7/12/82, p. 20*)

College Performance, Explanation of by Students

Males: Good grades are due to talent and ability.
Females: Good grades are due to effort.

(*Parlee, p. 65*)

College Students

Males: 48 percent of college students are male.
Females: 52 percent of college students are female. There are about half a million more women than men in the total college student body of 12.3 million.

(*Bird, p. 106, from the "Digest of Educational Statistics Census" in* Working Woman, *9/80, p. 74*)

College Students, Treatment of by Faculty
Men make more eye contact with professors, are called on more frequently, are favored as assistants, and are taken more seriously by professors than are female students.
("Let's Put Our Heads Together," p. 19)

Colonels
In 1980, out of 13,938 colonels in the armed services, 235 were female.
(Hacker, p. 206)

Color Blindness
Males: Men are afflicted with color blindness ten times more often than women are. Two to eight percent of all men are colorblind. Red and green blindness occurs only in men.
Females: Color blindness seems to be inherited from the maternal side, but is rare in women.
(Man's Body, pp. C17–19)

Combat Duty
All branches of the armed services prohibit women from serving in combat roles.
(Ross and Barcher, p. 280)

Comedians
Both males and females prefer male comedians.
(Hassett and Houlihan, p. 70)

Communications, Management in
31.3 percent of the management in the communications fields is female.
(Field, p. 78)

Competition at Work Between the Sexes
At work, men tend to be less ethical and harder on women than they are with men.
(Wagenvoord/Bailey, Men, p. 255)

Competitiveness
Male: Men are competitive against each other and against achievers of either sex.
Female: Women are competitive against each other and against nonachievers of either sex.
(*Mitchell, p. 112*)

Composers
There are more male than female composers.
(Newsweek, *5/18/81, p. 81*)

Computer Camps
There are three boys for every girl enrolled in computer camps.
(*Kiesler, Sproull, and Eccles, p. 42*)

Computer Information Sciences
In 1980, only 30 percent of all college graduates specializing in computer information sciences were female.
(Graduate Women, *cover page, unnumbered*)

Computers, Talking
Talking computers are being used to associate females with low service jobs and males with high status jobs. Males' voices are being used in "calculators, computers, and emergency calling devices." Women's voices are being used for "supermarket checkouts, scanners, telephone information systems, and vending machines."
(*Griffin quoting Steven LeVeen from* The New York Times, *p. M-2*)

Computer Science, Doctorates
Male: 90.4 percent of the computer science doctorates awarded during the academic year 1979–80 went to men.
Female: 9.6 percent were awarded to women.
(*Hacker, p. 244*)

Conceited
Men are said to be more conceited than women.
(*Eppingham, p. 37*)

Conception and Birth
About 120 males are conceived for every 100 females. 105 boys are born for every 100 girl babies.
(Good Looks, *12/81, p. 20*)

Conductor's Guild Membership
Ten percent of the 400 members of the Conductor's Guild are women.
(*Scott*, Parade, *1/8/84, p. 2*)

Conflict Resolution
Males: Men often resolve serious conflict by using physical aggression.
(*Wagenvoord/Bailey*, Women, *p. 24*)
Females: Women usually resolve conflict by verbal means.
(*Wagenvoord/Bailey*, Men, *p. 21*)

Control of Sex Hormones
The hypothalamus gland in the brain releases a hormone that controls sex hormones in both men and women.
(*Wagenvoord/Bailey*, Men, *p. 21*)

Conversations
In conversations between men, the exchanges are more topical than are conversations between women, in which exchanges are usually on a more personal and relational level.
(*Davidson and Duberman, p. 811*)
Studies show that when men and women are together, men do more of the talking, and are more likely to interrupt than women are.
(*Davis, p. 98*)

Conversations, Mothers with Infants
Some studies show that mothers talk and sing more with their girl babies than with their boy babies.
(Newsweek, *5/18/81, p. 73*)

Cooking, When Both Parents Work
Although 51 percent of the households surveyed felt that the cooking chore should be shared equally, 75 percent of the house-

holds admitted that the woman does the cooking, with only 25 percent sharing the task. Men did the majority of the cooking in only 2 percent of the households.

(Keeley, p. 25)

Coronary Heart Disease, Age and

Male: Coronary heart disease is the leading cause of death among men over the age of forty.

Female: Coronary heart disease is the leading cause of death for women over age fifty-five.

(Fox, p. 10)

Estrogens and high-density lipoproteins protect premenopausal women as they lower the level of fats that can clog arteries, but with the reduction of estrogens after menopause, a woman loses her protection against heart disease, and the risk of heart attack becomes only slightly less than that of a man. However, a woman will recover from heart disease faster than a man will.

(S. Hammer, p. 22; Foley, p. 59)

Coronary Heart Disease and Diabetes

Males: Diabetic men have two to three times more heart disease than nondiabetic men.

Females: Diabetic women have five to six times more heart disease than nondiabetic women.

(Murray, Program Your Heart for Health, p. 98, 106; Kunz, p. 374)

Corporate Directors

Only 2 percent of corporate directors are female.

(Porter, p. 22)

Corporate Executives Earning $100,000 or More

Fifteen of the 2,500 corporate executives making $100,000 or more per year are female.

(Field, p. 78)

Corpus Callosum

The bridge between the two halves of the brain is called the corpus callosum. It is larger in women than in men and scientists speculate that the better communication between the brain halves in women may be due to the larger bridge, which gives "more room for neural pathways."

   (S. Hammer, p. 25)

Corrective Lenses

Male: 42.7 million men wear corrective lenses.
Female: 53.6 million women wear corrective lenses.

   (U.S. Statistical Abstract, p. 121)

Craftsman, Machine Operator, Nonfarm Laborer

Males: Forty-five percent of the men in the labor force work as craftsmen, machine operators, or nonfarm laborers.
Females: Fourteen percent of the women in the labor force work at these jobs.

   (Cornfield, Psychology Today, December 1983, p. 19)

Creative Writing Courses

Women outnumber men in creative writing courses.

   (Bird, p. 788)

Creativity

The only differences in creative ability are that women tend to excel in verbal areas, and men in spatial.

   (Guilford, p. 232; Goleman, p. 59)

Crime

The majority of all types of crimes are committed by men. Only one out of five serious crimes (murder, arson, and robbery) is committed by a woman. However, the rates of women's involvement in nonviolent crime is rising. For instance, the rate of embezzlement among women has risen 24 percent since 1979.

   (Murphy, p. 50)

Crime-stopping

In one study, 25 percent more women than men tried to stop a thief.

   (Researcher: William Austin, University of Virginia, p. 28; Cory, April 1980, p. 28)

Criminally Insane, Most Common Diagnosis of
Males: Antisocial personality is the most common diagnosis of the males found to be criminally insane.
Females: Schizophrenia is the most common diagnosis of females considered to be criminally insane.
(Human Behavior, *December 1977, p. 50*)

Criminal Offenders, Federal Institutions for
Males: There are twenty-three federal prisons for men.
Females: There are six federal prisons for females.
(Bird, p. 153)

Criminals and the Insanity Plea
Women are almost twice as likely as men to be judged insane and incompetent to stand trial.
(Human Behavior, *February 1977, p. 50; Researchers: Marijan Keyanis, M.D., Robert Vanderpool, M.D., Fritz Heam, Ph.D., University of Iowa)*

Crisis, Reaction to
Women are more irritated by small things than men are, but are more likely to remain calm and cool during a crisis.
(Eppingham, p. 37)

Crying
Males: In a University of Minnesota study on crying, 55 percent of men reported crying at least once during a one-month period. When they cried, it usually involved a welling of tears. Seventy-three percent of the men said they felt better after crying.
Females: Women cry five times as often as men. Ninety-four percent of women reported in the same study that they cried at least once or more during the one-month period. Women averaged five crying spells a month and when they cried, they sobbed or had flowing tears. Eighty-five percent of the women studied said they felt better after crying.

In both sexes the average crying time was one to two minutes. Crying usually occurs from about 7 to 10 P.M., while with relatives, watching a movie, or with friends.
(Researcher: William Frey, M.D., Kotulak, p. A13)

Crying, Method of
Males: Men are apt to report watery eyes as an excuse for flowing tears when crying.
Females: Women are more apt to say that they feel "lumps in their throat."

Both men and women cry for a duration of about six minutes, and both feel better after crying.

(*Squires, p. B3*)

Curiosity of Infants
Boy infants are more curious than girl infants and tend to enjoy taking things apart.

(Newsweek, 5/18/81, p. 73)

Cutters and Loggers
Ninety-nine percent of the cutters and loggers are male.

(*Hacker, p. 127*)

Cystitis (Inflammation of the bladder)
Cystitis afflicts more women than men.

(Woman's Body, p. 367)

Daydreams

Problem-solving and sex are two favorite themes of both male and female daydreamers. Sexual daydreams are more common in men than in women, except between the ages of thirty to thirty-four, when women have as many sex daydreams as men. The tendency to daydream decreases as we get older, although there is usually a spurt at middle age.

(Horn, October 1977, pp. 45, 46)

Deanships at Colleges

Women hold 18 percent of the deanships in four-year colleges.

(Psychology Today, September 1979, p. 77)

Death, Accidental

Males: Males are the victims of 69 percent of all accidental deaths.
Females: Females are the victims of 31 percent of all accidental deaths.

(Man's Body, p. 53–55)

Death, Sudden

Men are victims of sudden death three times more often than are women.

(Engel, p. 118)

Death, Thoughts of a Spouse's Possible Death
Males: Men most often fear that murder or suicide will be the cause of their spouse's death.
Females: More women than men think about their mate's possible demise. Women worry most about accidents or natural death as possible causes of their spouse's demise.

(*Researcher: Roberta Bear*, Psychology Today, *November 1981, p. 22*)

Death by Falling
Male: 7,325 men died as a result of falling in 1977. This was 51.8 percent of the total number of deaths by falling.
Female: 6,811 women died by falling. This is 48.2 percent of the total.

(*Hacker, p. 71*)

Death by Fire
Male: 3,878 men died as a result of fire in 1977. This is 61.2 percent of the total 8,338.
Female: 2,461 women died as a result of fire. This is 38.8 percent of the total.

(*Hacker, p. 72*)

Death by Firearms
Males: Males are the victims of 86 percent of all firearms deaths.
Females: Females are the victims of only 14 percent of all firearms deaths.

(Man's Body, *pp. 53–55*)

Death by Legal Intervention
(Deaths caused by law enforcement officers)
Male: In 1977, 289 men died as a result of legal intervention.
Female: 5 women died as a result of legal intervention.

(*Hacker, p. 73*)

Death by Poisoning in 1977
Male: 3,915 men died by poisoning. This is 68.3 percent of the total of 5,730.
Female: 1,815 women died by poisoning, or 31.7 percent of the total.

(*Hacker, p. 72*)

Death Due to Medical Complications and "Misadventures"
(Misadventures include anesthesia, drugs, X rays, or complications from diagnosis procedures.)
Male: In 1977, 1,669 men died from medical "misadventures."
Female: 1,340 women died from medical "misadventures."
  (*Hacker, p. 72*)

Death Due to Motor Vehicle Accidents in 1977
Male: 72.4 percent (34,049) of those who died in motor vehicle accidents were men.
Female: 27.6 percent (12,989) of those dying in a motor accident were women.
  (*Hacker, p. 71*)

Death Due to Water Transport Accidents in 1977
Male: 90.2 percent (1,237) of deaths due to water transport accidents were men.
Female: 134 women (or 9.8 percent) died in water transport accidents.
  (*Hacker, p. 71*)

Death of a Spouse and Adaptation
There are numerous studies pointing to the theory that the death of a spouse is more devastating for males than for females. While the incidence of cancer is higher among widows, their death rates are the same as for married women. However, death rates for widowers are much higher than they are for married men. (If a widower remarries, he then resumes the healthier married male record!)
  (*Bernard, pp. 20, 21*)

Death Penalty Approval or Disapproval
Sixty-two percent of women, in contrast to 72 percent of men, favor the death penalty for those convicted of murder.
  (*Tobias and Leader, p. 122*)

Death Rate of Infants
Males: 15.3 male infants per 1,000 die in the first few months of life.

Females: 12.9 girls per 1,000 die in the first few months of life.
(*Brothers,* Woman's Day, 2/9/82, p. 60)

Death Row (Awaiting Execution in 1980)
There were a total of 714 prisoners awaiting death in 1980. Of those, 706 were male and 8 were female.
(*Hacker,* p. 230)

Death Statistics in 1980
54.3 percent of all those who died in 1980 were male. 45.7 percent were female. One percent of all American males died in 1980, and .79 percent of American women died.
(*Hacker,* p. 66)

Decision Making
Women make decisions faster than men.
(*Ford,* p. 110)

Defense, Increased Spending on
"Women are far less likely than men to favor increased spending on defense (and also more likely to express no opinion)."
(*Tobias and Leader,* p. 122)

Degrees, Bachelor of Arts
Males: Men earn 54 percent of all bachelor of arts degrees.
Females: Women earn 46 percent of all bachelor of arts degrees.
(*Census, 1980,* p. 166)

Degrees, Master's
Males: Men earn 53 percent of all master's degrees.
Females: Women earn 47 percent of all master's degrees.
(*Census, 1980,* p. 166)

Degrees, PH.D.
Males: Men earn 70.5 percent of all doctoral degrees.
Females: Women earn 29.5 percent of all doctoral degrees.
(*Hacker,* p. 242)

Delinquency
Delinquency is five times more prevalent among boys than among girls.
(Sexton, p. 74)

Dental Assistants
98.6 percent of dental assistants are female.
(Hacker, p. 127)

Dental Degrees
Male: In the 1979–80 academic year, 86.5 percent of degrees in dentistry were awarded to men.
Female: 13.5 percent were awarded to women.
(Hacker, p. 244)

Dental-School Students
Twenty percent of the 4,457 students in the nation's sixty dental schools are female.
(Shearer, Parade Magazine, 12/25/83, p. 8)

Dentists
98.3 percent of dentists are male.
(Department of Labor, 1979)

Dentists, Perception of
Female dentists are perceived as happier, more understanding, and warmer than male dentists. They are also felt to be equal in terms of competence, independence, and self-reliance.
(Health, September 1983, p. 65)

Dentists, Visits to
Male: In 1979, 44.2 percent of the visits to dentists were made by men. They averaged 1.3 visits per year.
Female: 55.8 percent of the visits to dentists were made by women. They averaged 1.8 visits a year.
(Hacker, p. 79)

Depression
Women suffer from depression more than men do. Twice as many women as men are diagnosed as being severely depressed,

with the highest rates of depression occurring between the ages of twenty-one and thirty-five.

However, some say it may be that just as many men as women are depressed, but do not report it. Women do report more depressive symptoms, and two thirds of the forty million people reporting depression are female.

(What Everyone Should Know About Depression, p. 4)

Depression and Admittance to Hospitals
For every 175 women admitted to a hospital for depression, only 100 men are admitted.

(DeRosis and Pellagrino, p. 3)

Depression and College Students, Methods of Coping
Males: College men cope with depression by using drugs, sex, aggression, and ignoring the problem.
Females: College women cope by crying, overeating, undereating, drinking coffee, smoking, and seeking support from others.

(Kleinke, Staneski, and Mason, pp. 887, 888)

Depression and Treatment in Outpatient Clinics
For every 100 men, 238 women are treated for depression on an outpatient basis.

(DeRosis and Pellegrino, p. 3)

Depression When Children Come of Age and Leave Home
Men suffer more than women when the children leave home.

(Brothers, Woman's Day, 1/12/82, p. 50)

Development, Physical
Generally, males are slower to develop than females are. Until about the age of sixteen, when puberty is usually completed in the males, the growth rate of males is about 80 percent of the female growth rate.

(Farnham-Diggory, p. 37)

Diabetes
(A chronic disease of the pancreas in which the body cannot make use of nutrients in the normal manner.)

Women are 50 percent more likely to have diabetes than men, and more women than men die from diabetes.
(Ha'ilono Kīna, *November 1981, Vol. 24*)

Diabetes Among Juveniles
Young females are more likely to contract diabetes than are young males.
(*Interview with Perry Heintz, M.D.*)

Diet, Relationship to Cancer
Males: Forty-one percent of all cancers in men are related to poor diet.
Females: Sixty-one percent of all cancers in women are related to poor diet.
(Nutrition News, *1981, No. 8*)

Dieting
Women go on diets 50 percent more often than men.
(*Ubell, p. 13*)

Dieting and Spouse Support
Dieting women get more help with dieting from their spouses than they give.
(*Ubell, p. 13*)

Diet Pills
Males: Twenty percent of diet-pill users are men.
Females: Eighty percent of diet-pill users are female.
(*Frankfort, p. 96*)

Directness in Communication
Male: Men are more direct in communicating with others, and are less concerned about hurt feelings than are women.
Female: Women tend to communicate more indirectly than men, and are more concerned about not hurting someone's feelings.
(*Ford, p. 111*)

Disabled
There are slightly more disabled men than disabled women. (One third of the disabled are over age sixty-five.)
(*Man's Body, pp. C01–04*)

Disabled with Paid Employment
Male: Sixty percent of disabled men have paid employment.
Female: Twenty-nine percent of disabled women have paid employment.
(Bird, p. 104, from Jobs for the Disabled, *Levitan and Taggart, 1977*)

Disclosure
Women disclose more about themselves than do men.
(Davidson and Duberman, p. 811)

Discrimination in Pay
Women earn about 40 percent less than men do even though women have shown that they can and do perform as well as men.
(Norman, p. 70)

Discrimination in Seeking Jobs in Accounting
When applying for a job as an accountant, men are more successful than women in getting through the initial screening stage.
(Firth, p. 900)

Distraction by Novel Objects
Males are more easily distracted by novel objects than are females, starting in the crib.
(Coleman, p. 59)

Division of Labor When Both Partners Work
In a recent survey of households, the researcher reported that 75 percent of the wives prepared meals (with the other 25 percent sharing the chore), 58 percent of the husbands took out the garbage, and 42 percent shared the chore. Most of those interviewed felt husbands should pay the bills, and that wives should stay home with ill children. Meeting with teachers and child discipline were considered jobs for both parents.
(Keeley, 2/84, p. 25)

Divorce and Remarriage
Males: Eighty-three percent of divorced men remarry. Half of the divorced men who do remarry do it within the first three years after the divorce.
Females: Seventy-five percent of divorced women remarry.
(Foreman, p. 17C)

Divorce of Spouse for One Million Dollars
Males: Twenty percent of those surveyed said, "Yes, I would divorce my spouse for one million dollars!"
Females: Ten percent of those who were surveyed said they would divorce their spouse for one million dollars.
(Psychology Today, *survey, May 1981, p. 29*)

Dominance in Groups
In groups, dominance is usually held by a male.
(*Parlee, p. 65*)

Dominance in Home and School
Preschool boys are more dominant at home and at school than are preschool girls. Children from about eight to twelve perceive the parent of the same sex to be dominant. High school boys are dominant over high school girls. Wives become more dominant the longer the marriage continues.
(*Mitchell, pp. 108, 110*)

Dominance in Jobs
Women respond more intently to authority, and particularly to female authority, than men do.
(*Mitchell, pp. 118*)

Dominance in the University Classroom
Males: Men dominate a university classroom whenever the instructor is a male.
Females: Females are more assertive in a female-taught classroom.
(*Researchers: Sarah Sternglantz and Shirley Ficeh, State University of New York*)

Draft
Both sexes can be drafted, as there is nothing in the U.S. Constitution that would prevent Congress from drafting women if it chose to do so.
(*Ross and Barcher, p. 280*)

Dreams, Contents of
Males: Men are said to dream more about strangers and violence than women do. They dream about men twice as much as they

dream about women. When they do dream about women, it is usually related to sex.

Females: Females dream mostly of being indoors or of being in familiar settings. Interactions in dreams are friendly except prior to menstruation, when dreams may be filled with hostility, frustration, and anxiety. At ovulation, women's dreams are said to be calm and content, concerning achievement and peace. Women dream about both sexes equally.

(Men: A Book for Women, *Wagenvoord/Bailey,* p. 115)

Dressmakers
97.2 percent of dressmakers are female.

(*Hacker,* p. 127)

Drivers, Accident Rates
Female drivers are more cautious than male drivers, but the accident rates of both sexes are just about equal. The accident rates for women have been rising for the past twenty years, while those for men have been dropping.

(*Crosstalk,* Psychology Today, *January 1983,* p. 56)

Drug Overdose
More women than men overdose on drugs. The most common drugs involved in emergency room drug treatment are Valium, aspirin, Dalmane, Darvon, Elavil, and Librium.

(*Levy,* p. 197)

Drugs, Prescribed
Males: One third of all drugs are prescribed for men.

Females: Two thirds of all drugs are prescribed for women. Seventy-five percent of all drugs prescribed for women are antidepressants. Valium is the most frequently prescribed drug.

(*Bird,* p. 126)

Drunkenness
Women get drunk faster than men because they are lighter and have less water in their systems to dilute alcohol. Also, a woman who drinks just prior to menstruation, when her estrogen levels are low, gets drunk more easily and can become more nauseated with more difficult hangovers than during the rest of the cycle.

(*Jones and Parsons,* p. 57)

Dumb, Playing
More men than women play dumb at their jobs. However, more women play dumb with their husbands than vice versa.
(*Hughs and Gove, p. 74*)

Dupuytren's Contracture
(This condition is characterized by a thickening of the tissues under the skin of the palms of the hands, which can result in paralysis of the hands. Movement can be retained if the patient is operated on in the early stages of the disease.)
    This condition is found mainly in men.
(*Gardner, p. 88*)

Dyslexia
(This is a neurologically based language disorder, responsible for reading difficulties in which letters are confused, or perceived to be upside down.)
    Males are affected with dyslexia six times more often than females.
(*Farnham-Diggory, p. 131*)

Earnings, Lifetime, Increased by a College Education

Male: Men with a college degree increase their lifetime earnings by an average $329,000 over those who do not have a college degree.

Female: Women with a college degree earn about $142,000 more in a lifetime than women who do not have a college degree. Women with a college degree earn only 60 percent of what male high school graduates earn.

(*Shearer, p. 8; Kantel, p. 5*)

Earnings Gap

The earnings gap between men and women is greatest in the professions historically held by men, such as medicine, and smallest in professions held by women, such as teaching.

(*Murphy, p. 50*)

Earnings of Spouses

In one of ten American working couples, the wife earns more than the husband.

(*Rubinstein, p. 36*)

Education, Compensatory Title 1 for the Disadvantaged

(Title 1 is a federally sponsored program to provide financial assistance for extra school activities, such as camping or special excursions for school children, and is administered through state departments of education.)

Sixty percent of the families that are able to utilize Title 1 services are headed by women.
(Ehrenreich and Stallard, p. 221)

Educational Achievement of Men and Women Age 20 to 21
Male: In 1980, of 3,918,000 men of twenty to twenty-one years of age, 18 percent did not graduate from high school. Of the remaining 82 percent, 30.4 percent of those went to college. The remaining did not.
Female: Of 4,182,000 women, ages twenty to twenty-one, 15.6 percent failed to finish high school. Of the remaining 84.4 percent, 27.8 percent went to college and 56.6 percent did not.
(Hacker, p. 249)

Elderly, Institutions for
Three quarters of the elderly living in institutions are women.
(Bird, p. 153)

Electricians
98.8 percent of electricians are male.
(Hacker, p. 127)

Embryonic Tissue and Sexual Organ Development in the Fetus
In the fetus the same type of tissue develops into either the outer lips of the vagina, or the scrotum, depending on the balance of hormonal output and whether the fetus develops into a male or a female.
(Woman's Body, p. 415)

Emotional Difficulty
Women report more emotional difficulty than do men.
(Bernard, p. 80)

Emotional Disturbance in Adults in Psychiatric Hospitals
Males: Men in psychiatric hospitals are often assaultive, with records of robbery or rape, and histories of drunkenness.
Females: Women in psychiatric hospitals are more often depressed and prone to suicide attempts.
(DeRosis and Pellegrino, p. 3)

Empathy
Women are considered more empathetic than men.

(Psychology Today, *November 1978, p. 59*)

Emphysema
More men than women have emphysema, a condition in which the air spaces in the lungs are enlarged and breathing becomes difficult. It can eventually damage the heart.

(Brothers, Woman's Day, *2/9/82, p. 138*)

Employment
Males: In 1980, 64.6 percent of the men who worked did so full-time. 35.4 percent of the male workforce was employed part-time.

Females: 44.3 percent of the women who worked did so full-time. 55.7 percent worked less than full-time.

(Hacker, *p. 10*)

Employment, Full- and Part-time
Male: In 1980, 55,989,000 men were employed.

Female: In 1980, 41,281,000 women were employed.

(Hacker, *p. 128*)

Employment, Full-time
Male: In 1970, 41,881,000 men held full-time jobs.

Female: 22,859,000 held full-time jobs.

(Hacker, *p. 148*)

In 1980, a total of 72,023,000 persons were employed full-time.

Male: 62.2 percent were men.

Female: 37.8 percent were female.

(Hacker, *p. 119*)

Employment, Full-time, and Marital Status
In 1980, 45 percent of the workforce (32,390,000 men) was made up of married men. 20.7 percent of the workforce (14,913,000 women) was made up of married women. Twelve percent of the workforce (8,646,000 men) was made up of single men. Nine percent of the workforce (6,484,000 women) was made up of single women. 5.2 percent of the workforce (3,739,000) was made up of

separated, widowed or divorced men. 8.1 percent of the work-force (5,851,000) was made up of separated, widowed, or di-vorced women.

(Hacker, p. 119)

Endurance in Physical Activities
Women have greater endurance than men, due to the higher per-centage of fat in their bodies.

(Hammer, p. 21; Selden, p. 52)

Endurance of Physical Stress
A woman's endurance under conditions such as starvation, ex-posure, stress, and shock, is better than a man's.

(Interview with Irving Marvit, M.D.)

Energy, Quick
Men have more quick energy than women, as they have greater total amounts of stored, quick fuels known as phosphocreatine and glycogen, and more oxygen in their bloodstreams.

(Brothers, Woman's Day, 2/9/82, p. 138; Hammer, p. 21)

Energy Reserves
Women have more long-term energy reserves than men because their bodies are made up of a higher percentage of fat, and fat burns slowly.

(Hammer, p. 21; Selden, p. 52)

Energy Use on the Job
Women expend 12 percent more energy on the job than men do.

(Researchers: University of Michigan, Institute of Social Research; Fogg, p. 18)

Engineering, Master's Degrees in
Male: In the 1979–80 academic year, 15,133 masters degrees in engineering were awarded to men.
Female: 1,142 were awarded to women.

(U.S. Statistics, p. 166)

Engineering Doctorates
Male: In the 1979–80 academic year, 96.4 percent of the doctor-ates were awarded to men.

Female: 3.6 percent of the doctorates were awarded to women.
(*Hacker, p. 244*)

Engineering School
Male: 89.6 percent of the graduates of engineering school are male.
Female: 10.4 percent of the graduates of engineering school are female.
(*Time, 7/12/82, p. 21*)

Engineers
Four percent of the engineers in the U.S.A. are female.
(*Shearer, p. 10*)
Ninety-six percent of engineers are male.
(*Hacker, p. 128*)

English Channel, Crossing of
Women swimmers have higher crossing speeds than men. (The fastest crossing was accomplished by fourteen-year-old Penny Dean of California, who beat the fastest male by three hours.)
(*Newsweek, 5/18/81, p. 73*)

English Majors in College
Seventy percent of those majoring in English are women.
(*Bird, p. 88*)

English Professors
Male: Ninety-three percent of English professors are men.
Female: Seven percent of English professors are women.
(*Bird, p. 88*)

Epstein-Barr Virus
This is a genetic disorder that causes a faulty immune response. Males with this disorder may develop infectious mononucleosis or cancer of the lymph glands. It is rare in females.
(Science Digest, *September 1982, p. 90*)

Erections, Morning and During Sleep
Both men and women experience erections (of the penis in men, and of the clitoris in women) during sleep or upon waking. This

is because the highest levels of testosterone (sexual-desire-stimu-
lating hormone) occur just before sunrise, with the lowest levels
occurring about 11 P.M. Erections are also associated with rapid
eye movement and can occur throughout the night, while
sleeping.

(*Murray, p. 263; Mitchell, p. 39*)

Erotic Material
Literature and films of an erotic nature are equally sexually stimulating to both sexes.

(*Heiman, p. 91*)

Escapes from Prison, 1980
During 1980, 6,052 prisoners escaped from state prisons; 382 of
those were women. Of the 5,540 prisoners who were returned,
367 were women.

(*Hacker, p. 229*)

Estrogens
Estrogens are primarily female sex hormones produced by the
ovaries and adrenal glands in women and, to a lesser degree, by
the testes and adrenal glands in men. Estrogens are not only
needed by the female to stimulate the growth of the lining of the
uterus, but also by both sexes for vital cell function. The amount
of estrogen a woman produces throughout her menstrual cycle
varies considerably, and she may have as much as one and a half
to eleven times as much as a man, depending on what part of her
cycle she is in. Estrogen levels rise sharply after ovulation and
during pregnancy. High levels of estrogen can result in wake-
fulness, irritability, headaches, and fluid retention in women.
There is a drop in estrogen at the onset of menses, childbirth,
and menopause, and some women feel depressed at these times.
Estrogens have been utilized in small doses in some men for the
treatment of arthritis, and infertility.

(*Money, p. 1837; Dranov, p. 32; Hammer, p. 22; Mitchell, p. 39*)

Estrogen, Source of after Menopause
Prior to menopause, a woman's estrogen comes primarily from
her ovaries. After menopause, it is derived from other, similar
hormones that can be transformed by the body into small

amounts of estrogen. After menopause the amount of estrogen in males and females is about equal.

(*Cooley, p. 443*)

Euthanasia

Male: One half of the male respondents to one survey said they had told a friend or a relative they would rather be dead than kept alive by a machine.
Female: Two thirds of the female respondents to the survey indicated they have revealed to a friend or relative that they would rather be dead than kept alive by a machine.

(*Rubinstein,* Psychology Today, *10/82, p. 30*)

Exaltolide

This is a chemical exuded by males with a musky smell that is contained in many perfumes.
Males: Men excrete twice as much exaltolide in their urine as women do.
Females: Women are much more sensitive to exaltolide than men are. This sensitivity heightens at the time of ovulation. Many authorities feel this has a particularly attractive effect, which may have served as a fertility cue in primeval times.

(*Hassett, p. 40*)

Executions

Between 1930 and 1980 there were 3,862 people executed in the United States. Of these, 32 were female.

(*Hacker, p. 231*)

Executives in Top Companies

Only 5 percent of the executives in the top U.S.A. companies are female.

(Time, *7/12/82, p. 20*)

Exercise

Almost as many women as men exercise.

(*Ubell, p. 13*)

Exercise, Capacity for and Aging
Males: At fifty-five a man has only 70 percent of the capacity to exercise that he had at twenty-five.
Females: A fifty-five-year-old woman's capacity for exercise is reduced by only 10 percent of her capacity at twenty-five.
(*Brothers, p. 25*)

Exhibitionism
Exhibitionist tendencies are more common among males than among females.
(*Kolb, p. 506*)

Expectations, Parental
Men perceive more parental support for their career goals than women do. The plans of the male are associated with the father's career, whereas females are under less pressure to follow parental footsteps.
(*Researchers: James Goodall, Ph.D., York University, Canada,* Human Behavior, *February 1977, p. 35*)

Exploratory Behavior
Males exhibit more exploratory behavior (starting at an early age as they move away from their mothers to explore the surrounding environment) than females do.
(*Sexton, pp. 74–75*)

Extramarital Intercourse
Men have more extramarital affairs than women do. One out of every two married men will have an affair, while only one out of five married women will do so, by the age of forty-five.
(*Hassett, p. 37*)

Eye Contact
Females are superior at making and maintaining eye contact, beginning in the cradle.
(*Newsweek, 5/18/1981, p. 73*)

Falling in Love
Men fall in love faster than women.
Males: Twenty-five percent fall in love by the first date.
Females: Fifteen percent fall in love by the fourth date.
   (Rubin, p. 56)

Falling out of Love
Women fall out of love more quickly than men.
   (Rubin, p. 56)

Falls, and Death by Falling, of the Aged
More women over seventy-five die from falling than do men of
the same age.
   (Cooley, p. 458)

Fasting
More men than women fast.
   (Ubell, p. 13)

Fat, Subcutaneous (Under the skin)
Women have about seven more pounds of "under the skin" fat
than men.
   (Klafs and Arnheim, p. 184)

Fat, Total
Males: Fifteen percent of a man's body is composed of fat.

Females: Twenty-seven percent of a woman's body is made up of fat.

(Newsweek, *5/18/81, p. 75*)

Fat and Wealth
Males: Rich men are fatter than poor men.
Females: Rich women are thinner than poor women.

(Kolb, *p. 462*)

Fatigue
Males: Men tire faster than women.
Females: Women tire more slowly than men unless they are iron deficient, when they may tire more easily than men.

(Selden, *p. 52*)

Fat Metabolism
Some authorities feel women burn fat more slowly and more efficiently than men.

(Selden, *p. 52*)

Fat Ratio
An adult female has twice as much fat as an adult man.

(Edelstein, *p. 12*)

Fat Storage
(Fat that serves as an insulating layer below the skin and around the internal organs, and as a nutritional reserve that is burned to produce energy during exercise.)
Males: Twelve percent of a man's body is composed of storage fat.
Females: Fifteen percent of a woman's body is storage fat.

(Stump, *p. 94*)

Fat Storage, Location of
Males: Men usually store extra fat in their abdomens.
Females: Women usually store extra fat in their hips, upper arms, breasts, and thighs.

(Wagenvoord/Bailey, *Men, p. 206*)

Felonies

In 1975, 16 percent of the serious crimes in the U.S.A. were committed by women. That year the proportion of women who committed larceny and theft was 500 percent higher, and the rate of women charged with embezzlement and fraud was 300 percent higher, than in 1953.

(Human Behavior, *November 1978, p. 12*)

Fertility and Aging

Males: Men usually retain their fertility into old age.
Females: Women lose their fertility after menopause, when they are about fifty years old.

(Cooley, p. 27)

Fertility and Heat

Males: Male fertility drops when their genitals are exposed to high temperatures.

(Wagenvoord/Bailey, Men, p. 126)

Females: Female fertility is highest when the room temperature is 64 degrees Fahrenheit.

(Glassman, p. 76)

Fetal Development

For the first six weeks following conception, all fetuses are essentially the same and indistinguishable. By about the sixth week, if the embryo is genetically "programmed" to be male, the Y chromosome transforms a certain cluster of cells (called the primordial gonad) into testes. They then begin to produce male hormones, especially testosterone. If the fetus is to be female, nothing happens until about the twelfth week, when the female system begins to produce the ovarian hormones estrogen and progesterone.

(Wagenvoord/Bailey, Woman, pp. 19/20)

Fetuses and Survival

Female fetuses are more likely to survive than male fetuses. Male fetuses are more likely to survive if conceived during September or November.

(Glassman, p. 76)

Fighting
Men fight more than women. This seems to be true for males of most species. (Many authorities cite this as an adjunct to the consensus that men are more aggressive.)
(*Newsweek, 5/18/1981, p. 74*)

Financial Security
Men appear to be more confident and self-assured about finances than women.
(*Psychology Today Survey, May 1981; Rubinstein, p. 39*)

Fine Coordination (Control of the small muscles, such as in the fingers)
Women have better fine coordination than men.
(*Newsweek, 5/18/81, p. 81; Psychology Today, November 1978, p. 59*)

Fingerprints
The ridges of a woman's fingerprints are narrower and more uniform than a man's.
(*"Update," Science Digest, September 1981, p. 24*)

Fingers, Length of
Males: The index finger of a man is longer than his ring finger.
Females: The ring finger of a woman is longer than her index finger.
(*Wagenvoord/Bailey, Men, p. 60*)

Fingertips
A woman's fingertips are usually more sensitive than a man's.
(*Gottlieb, p. 82*)

Fire Fighters
Male: 179,550 of the paid firemen in the United States are men.
Female: 450 are women.
(*Greenberger, p. 23; Hacker, p. 127*)

Flexibility
Women are more flexible physically than men, due to the higher levels of estrogen in their bodies.
(*Selden, p. 53*)

Flexitime
Males: One of seven men work flexible hours.
Females: One of ten women work flexible hours.
(*Nollen, p. 153*)

Flowers, Ordering and Sending of
Women both order and send more flowers than men do.
(*James, p. 11*)

Follicle-Stimulating Hormone (or FSH)
Males: In men this hormone causes sperm production.
Females: In women this hormone causes an egg cell to mature in preparation for ovulation.
(*Cooke and Dworkin, p. 103*)

Food, Need for
Men need more food than women of equal weight (women burn fewer calories per pound than men because they have less muscle per pound).
(*Selden, p. 52*)

Food Stamps
Eighty-five percent of the 22 million people who receive food stamps are women and children.
(*Ehrenreich and Stallard, p. 220*)

Friendships
Men have more friendships early in life and women have more after middle age.
(*Researcher: Claude Fisher, University of California at Berkeley; Psychology Today, Horn, November 1980, p. 28*)
Men seem to have more friends than women, but the friendships of the women are more intimate, spontaneous, and affectionate.
(*Davidson and Duberman, p. 811*)
Women seek long-term friendships with both sexes. Men, single or married, tend to stay away from friendships with women as they seem to feel they cannot have a real relationship with a woman unless there is sexual involvement.
(*Phillips, p. 19, in Woman*)

Fun and Attractiveness
Attractive men have more fun than attractive women.

(Jones, Section C, p. 1)

Funny
Men try harder to be funny than women do. Authorities feel that women are not trained to be funny. In one study involving group therapy sessions, men were five times more likely to be funny than women were.

(Hassett and Houlihan, p. 70)

G

Gallstones

(Particles resembling stones that form in the gallbladder—the reservoir where bile, a waste product, is formed—are called gallstones. These stones are made up of various substances such as cholesterol and bilirubin, a substance formed by the breakdown of hemoglobin from old red blood cells. At times, if the balance of these substances becomes upset, a tiny solid particle forms in the gallbladder. Between one half and one third of those 20 million who have gallstones never know it as there are no symptoms, but if the stone moves into the narrow cystic duct, it can cause spasms with severe pain in the region of the gallbladder. Older people are at higher risk for developing gallstones than younger ones. One in five elderly people have gallstones.)

Male: Men over forty have a 20 percent chance of developing gallstones and 8 percent of all men have them.

Female: If a woman is over forty, there is a fifty-fifty chance she will have gallstones. Autopsy studies show that 20 percent of all women have gallstones.

(*Cooley, p. 211; Kunz, p. 489*)

Garbage Collectors

97.1 percent of garbage collectors are male.

(*Hacker, p. 127*)

Gastroenteritis

Gastroenteritis is an inflammation of the stomach and the intestines. More men than women suffer from this disease.

(*Brothers, Woman's Day, 2/9/82, p. 138*)

Generals
In 1980, of 1,111 generals, only 6 were female.
(Hacker, p. 206)

Genes, Abnormal
Men have more abnormal genes than women because of their
unmatched X and Y chromosomes. It is rare for a woman, who
has two matching X chromosomes, to inherit a defective gene.
(Man's Body, pp. C17–19)

Gonadotropins
Gonadotropins are the male and female hormones produced by
the pituitary gland that trigger the release of other hormones.
There are two major gonadotropins: (1) the follicle-stimulating
hormone stimulates the growth of the follicle, which contains
the ovum that produces estrogen in females. It also stimulates
the production of sperm in males; (2) the luteinizing hormone
stimulates ovulation in the female. The same hormone, called
ICSH, interstitial cell stimulating hormone, is responsible for the
production of testosterone and other male hormones.
(Mitchell, p. 12)

Gonads
The name for the sex glands; the testes in men and the ovaries in
women.
(Hammer, p. 19)

Gonorrhea
Gonorrhea is a venereal disease caused by a bacteria that thrives
in the warm moisture of the urethra, vagina, rectum, or mouth. It
occurs in one of five people under twenty.
Males: In men, the incubation period (the time lapse between the
infection and the appearance of symptoms) is about a week. The
symptoms are a thick discharge, pain upon urination and discomfort inside the penis. The test for gonorrhea in males is 99
percent reliable. When gonorrhea goes undetected in males, it
may cause damage to the urethra, and sterility.
Females: Women are five to ten times more susceptible than men
to contracting gonorrhea if exposed, and the incubation period
for them is much longer. There are no distinct symptoms in 80

percent of women. The other 20 percent may have only a slight discharge resembling a minor infection, and the disease may go undetected until it is at an advanced stage. If the female is infected, she needs twice the amount of penicillin a man does.

Complications of the disease in women include infection of the fallopian tubes, which can lead to scarring and sterility, and acute infection in the abdomen. A woman who is pregnant can infect her baby as it passes through the birth canal, and it can become blind unless treated. If the gonorrhea bacterium gets into an adult's (male or female) eyes, it can cause blindness.

(*Cooke & Dworkin, pp. 334–335*)

Gonorrhea, Rates
Males: In 1980 there were 538.8 reported cases of gonorrhea per 100,000 men.
Females: There were 353.1 reported cases for every 100,000 women.

(*Hacker, p. 78*)

Gossip
The majority of adults surveyed feel that men and women gossip an equal amount.

(*"Let's Put Our Heads Together," p. 25*)

Gout
(Gout is a metabolic disorder in which the body tends to accumulate uric acid. The acid builds up, causing a painful inflammation of joints. It is associated with aging.)
Males: Ninety-three percent of the 1 million victims of gout are men. They rarely contract it before age forty-five.
Females: Gout develops in women only after menopause.

(*Man's Body, pp. 28–31*)

Government, Jobs in
Women with identical educations and work experience as men earn less and have less expectation of advancement in government jobs. However, opportunities in government jobs are generally better than in industry.

(*Kantel, pp. 10, 11, 12*)

Government, Seats in
Male: In 1980, 88 percent of the elected government seats went to males.
Female: Twelve percent, or 16,000 women, held government posts. (This is up from 4 percent in 1975.)
   (Avery, p. 55)

Grades, High School Students
Boys begin making better grades than girls during high school.
   (Murphy, p. 50)

Graduate Degrees and Advancement
Women are rewarded far less than men for the career preparation represented by a graduate degree.
   (Kantel, p. 965; Porter, p. 22, Census, p. 167)

Graduate School
Males: In the 1982–83 academic year, 862,000 men were enrolled in graduate school.
Females: 709,000 women were enrolled in graduate school.
   (Murphy, p. 50)

Gram Stain
(A test for gonorrhea that involves taking a smear of the vaginal discharge in females, and the urethral discharge in males.)
Males: This test is 99 percent reliable for males.
Females: This test is not reliable in females unless the results are positive. However, if the results are negative (indicating that she does not have the disease), follow-up tests are administered, as the negative results are usually only about 20 percent accurate for a woman.
   (Frankfort, p. 127; Waikiki Health Center, V.D. Clinic)

Gray Matter
Gray matter, located in a quarter-inch layer at the surface of the brain, is basically responsible for intelligence. Neurologists at the University of Pennsylvania indicate that blood flows faster through gray matter than through any other brain tissue. By measuring the rate of blood flow, they determined the amount of gray matter available, and found that women and left-handed people

(male or female) have more gray matter than men who are right-handed. They did not speculate regarding the implications of this study.

(Science Digest, *December 1982, p. 94)*

Gross Motor Abilities

Men are more skilled at gross motor activities than women are.

(Goleman, p. 59)

Growth Spurts

Boys: Boys experience their most significant growth spurts at thirteen or fourteen, and their growth is complete by seventeen. Girls: In girls, the growth spurt peaks at age twelve and ends by fourteen or fifteen.

(Hammar, p. 11)

Hair
Hair is found on the surface of the entire body, except on the palms, the soles, and parts of the genitals on both sexes. In the male, there is more growth on the face than in the female.
(Woman's Body, p. 208)

Hair, Pubic
(Hair that surrounds the genitals is called pubic hair.)
In women, pubic hair grows in a horizontal line. In men, however, it grows up toward the navel.
(Wagenvoord and Bailey, Men, p. 84)

Hairdressers
Male: 11.7 percent of hairdressers are male.
Female: 88.3 percent of hairdressers are female.
(Hacker, p. 128)

Hair Growth and Aging
Males: Men actually become hairier as they age, not on the head but inside the nose and ears, and on the back.
Females: Women experience a thinning of the hair on the head and pubic area as they age.
(Cooke and Dworkin, p. 306)

Hair Loss
Both men and women lose some 100 hairs a day from the scalp. Most of a woman's hair grows back. Due to the activity of testos-

terone, however, men can become bald.
(Man's Body, *p. D28*)

Hair Loss, Reasons for
Ninety percent of baldness can be attributed to hereditary factors.
Males: Men can also lose their hair due to stress, protein or mineral deficiencies, insufficient unsaturated fatty acids, or high levels of testosterone and other androgens.
(Man's Body, *p. D34*)
Females: Women lose their hair for the same reasons as men (except for high levels of testosterone). They also lose it due to anemia, peroxides, tight hair curlers, hair straighteners, sprays and conditioners, and following pregnancy and birth. These losses are usually temporary.
(Woman's Body, *p. 213*)

Hairs, Color and Density of
A woman's hairs are less densely colored than a man's, and thinner.
(Wagenvoord/Bailey, Men, p. 61)

Hairs on the Body, Number of
Both men and women have the same number of body hairs.
(Wagenvoord/Bailey, Women, p. 64)

Handicaps, Chronic Conditions
Males: In 1978, 14,564,509 males were chronically handicapped.
Females: 15,610,553 females were chronically handicapped.
(Almanac, *1981, p. 145*)

Handkerchiefs, Purchases of Men's
Women buy nine out of ten men's handkerchiefs.
(Boyd, 11/18/83, p. A26)

Hands
Male: The average male hand is 19.7 cm in length.
Female: The average female hand is 17.3 cm in length.
(Human Behavior, *October 1977, p. 72*)

Handwriting
A man's handwriting will often be more assertive than a woman's. Some feel this is due to cultural conditioning. Others feel it is because men have ten times as much testosterone (the hormone associated with aggression) as women.
(Riddel, p. 23)

Happiness
Males: One third of the men in the U.S.A. consider themselves happy.
Females: One half of the women in the U.S.A. consider themselves happy.
(Gallup Poll in Brothers, Woman's Day, *1/12/82, p. 92)*

Happiness and the Marital State
Married men are said to be the happiest group of males. Single women rank second (even single working women with children rank higher on the happiness scale than married women with children). Married women rank third, with single men at the bottom of the happiness scale.
(Eppingham, p. 37)

Happiness and the Single Life
Single men are less happy and more dependent than single women; single women are happier, better adjusted, and more independent than single men.
("Let's Put Our Heads Together," p. 21)

Harvard Medical School
Male: Two thirds of the Harvard Medical School graduating class is male.
Female: One third of the graduating class is female.
(Time, 5/12/1982, p. 23)

Headaches
Women report twice as many headaches as men do.
(National Health Survey, McCall's, *February 1983, p. 76)*

Health Workers
(Nonprofessional workers such as nurses' aides in hospitals.)

Male: Thirty percent of all health workers are male.
Female: Seventy percent of health workers are female.
(*Frankfort, p 136*)

Healthy, Feeling
Men feel healthier than women. Females report more psychological difficulties, more overweight, and more stress.
(*Rubinstein, p. 32 [From the* Psychology Today *Survey, 1982]*)

Hearing
Males: On the average, men lose their hearing earlier than women do.
Females: Women can hear better than men but are less tolerant of loud noises and repetitive sounds. Sensitivity to sound persists throughout life for women.
(*Goleman, p. 59*)

Hearing Loss in Those over 65
Twenty to fifty percent of Americans over sixty-five have a hearing loss. Not only are men the most seriously afflicted, but hearing losses show up earlier in men than in women, and are more common.
(Health and Longevity Report, *11/15/83, p. 1*)

Heart Attacks
Males: Men have three times as many heart attacks as women. It is the most common cause of death among men after age sixty. One of every two men will die of heart disease.
(Nutrition News, *1981, Vol. IV, No. 8*)
A man has a one in five chance of having a heart attack after age sixty-five.
(*Man's Body, pp. 31–32*)
Females: Before age forty-five, women are the victims of only one of every eight heart attacks. After menopause, the rate of heart attacks among women increases dramatically.
(You and Your Heart, *p. 3; Pascoe, p. 90*)
Among men the likelihood of heart disease after age sixty-five is 2.2 times that of women. Two out of five women die of heart disease.
(*Murray,* Program Your Heart for Health, *p. 31*)

Heartbeats
Males: The average male heart beats seventy-two times per minute.
Females: The average female heart beats eighty times per minute.
(Wagenvoord/Bailey, Men, p. 84)
The male heart is five to eight beats per minute slower than the female because of its larger size.
(Klafs and Arnheim, p. 183)

Heart Disease, Death from
Male: 370.4 males per 100,000 died of heart disease in 1979.
Female: 297.9 females per 100,000 died of heart disease in 1979.
In 1950, the rates were 424.7 for males and 289.7 for females.
(Statistical Abstract of the U.S., *1982–83)*

Heart Disease and High Density Lipoprotein
In the body's system for carrying fats (which don't mix with water) through the watery bloodstream, it is the task of the proteins to carry cholesterol to cells where it is needed and to carry out excess cholesterol. Low density proteins carry the cholesterol to the cells and high density proteins (HDL) carry it out of the body. Within the past ten years researchers have accumulated strong evidence indicating that those with high levels of this protein in their blood are less likely to have heart attacks. One way of measuring one's risk is to determine the ratio of total cholesterol to HDL.
Males: In men, the average ratio is 5:0.
Females: In women, the average ratio is 4:5.
(The goal for men should be to reduce it to 4:5.)
("Medical Forum," Harvard Healthletter, November 1979, Vol. V, No. 1)

Heart Disease and Meat-eaters
Male: Middle-aged men who are meat-eaters are four times more likely to suffer a fatal heart attack than nonmeat-eaters. Older men (age fifty-five and up) are twice as likely to suffer a heart attack if they eat meat six or more times per week than those who do not eat meat.
Female: The risk of a fatal heart attack does not differ between meat- and nonmeat-eaters in young women. In older women, the

risk of dying of a heart attack is greater in meat-eaters than in nonmeat-eaters.
(*Brody*, p. A16)

Heart Size at Birth
The male infant's heart is larger than a female infant's.
(Man's Body, pp. A05–06)

Heart Weight and Size
Males: The male heart weighs about ten ounces, and is larger than that of the female.
Females: The female heart weighs about eight ounces.
(Man's Body, p. B14)

Heat
Males: In hot weather, men feel warmer than women.
Females: Women stay cooler in hot weather, as fat acts as an insulator.
(*Brothers*, Woman's Day, 2/9/82, p. 138)

Heberden's Nodes
(A form of osteoarthritis that is ten times more prevalent in women than in men.)
Women who are afflicted with Heberden's nodes are usually postmenopausal. Usually all the fingers are affected, causing an enlarging of the end joint and bony, hard nodules on the joints.
(*Cooley*, p. 241)

Height
Men are generally about 10 percent taller than women.
(*Wagenvoord/Bailey*, Men, p. 84)

Height/Weight Average
Males: The average male is five feet nine inches tall and weighs one hundred and sixty-two pounds.
Females: The average woman is five feet three and one half inches tall and weighs one hundred and thirty-five pounds.
(Man's Body, p. A19–21)

Hemoglobin Concentration
The mature male's hemoglobin concentration is two to three grams per 100 ml., or about 30 percent higher than the female's.
(Hammar, p. 7; Dyer, p. 110)

Hemophilia
This is a rare condition inherited from the maternal side, but usually seen only in the male. The disorder is characterized by uncontrollable bleeding, as one of the elements needed for blood clotting is missing. There are eight cases per 10,000 and three to four severe cases per 100,000.
(Dranov, p. 32)

Hernia, Femoral
Femoral hernias are most often seen in females. The passageway through which the main blood vessels pass from the abdomen to the leg is called the femoral canal. In a hernia, a part of the intestines passes down the canal and protrudes at the top of the leg.
(Man's Body, pp. C25–27)

Hernias, Inguinal
Inguinal hernias usually occur in males, and are accelerated by heavy manual labor. The inguinal canal is the passage down which the testes descend just before birth. In an inguinal hernia, a part of the intestines passes down the inguinal canal into the scrotum.
(Man's Body, pp. C25– 27)

Herpes
(Herpes is a venereal disease that is now a public health problem and allegedly one of several major reasons young adults are reducing their sexual activity and becoming more selective about it. Herpes can kill a baby if the child is born during a time when the herpes is active. There are 20 million people in the U.S.A. who have herpes.)
Fifty-one percent of herpes victims are female.
(Leo, p. 66)

Hiccups
Men have hiccups more often than women do.
(Ladies' Home Journal, February 1983, p. 51)

High Blood Pressure

Males: More men than women die from causes related to high blood pressure.

Females: There are more women than men who have high blood pressure.

For every four hypertensive men, there are five hypertensive women.

(*Murray, p. 64; Dustan [Pages unnumbered]*)

High School Students, Behavior, 1977

Males: Boys are reported to be more aggressive, with more suspensions and failures than females. Boys who receive good grades have higher self-esteem and less aggression than those that make poor grades.

Females: Girls are reported to experience more internal stress such as anxiety, depression, guilt, and psychosomatic complaints than boys. In terms of achievement, girls have to make "A" in order to boost self-esteem, in contrast to boys for whom a "B" is good enough.

(*Horn,* Psychology Today, *2/78, pp. 36 and 37*)

High School Students, Goals

Male: Recent studies of the goals of adolescents reveal that most high school boys wish for managerial or blue-collar jobs, and lots of money. More boys than girls do not want children.

Female: Girls look forward to clerical or teaching jobs, and finding the right man to marry. More girls than boys wish for four or more children.

(*Murphy, p. 51*)

High School Students, Jobs

Males: More boys than girls take after-school jobs. They work an average of 22.5 hours per week, making an average of $3.38 per hour.

Females: Girls work an average of 18.6 hours per week at their part-time jobs, and earn an average of $2.99 per hour.

(*Murphy, p. 51*)

Hips

A woman's hips are broader and shallower than those of a man, due to the activity of hormones. (Many feel the wider hips in

women are necessary to enable them to carry a baby, both inside and outside the body.)
(Murphy, p. 50; Selden, July 1981, p. 50)

History Books

A study by Janice Trecker, published by the National Council for Social Studies, states that topics like women's suffrage and birth control are given very little attention in history books. Trecker cites one example in which five pages were devoted to the story of the six-shooter and five lines to that of a frontierswoman.
(Bird, p. 107)

Homes for the Elderly

There are more women than men in retirement homes, due to the greater longevity of women.
(Bird, p. 127)

Homicide

More men than women commit murder.
(Brothers, Woman's Day, 2/9/82, p. 138)

Homicide Victims (1978)

Males:	White:	8,429
	Black:	7,118
Females:	White:	2,771
	Black:	1,739

(Census, 1980, p. 180)

Homosexuality

Males: Between 2 and 5 percent of the adult males in Western society can be called homosexual.
(Man's Body, pp. K26–27)
Females: It is estimated that between 2 and 5 percent of the female population is lesbian.
(Woman's Body, p. 49)

Hormonal Changes and Mood

Males: There has not been significant research into the correlation between mood changes and hormonal levels in males. It is known, however, that their testosterone levels change from day

to day and week to week, sometimes with regularity.
Females: Ninety percent of women's mood changes occur premenstrually. Depression is highest when estrogen levels are low. Elation and feelings of well being occur in women around the time of ovulation (mid-cycle), when estrogen levels are high.
(*Franks and Burtle, p. 31*)

Hormonal Changes During the Day
Both men and women experience hormonal shifts during the day, as the luteinizing hormone (which stimulates ovulation in women, and the production of testosterone and other androgens in men) is secreted in bursts every hour. Estrogen and testosterone levels are at their highest in the morning just after sunrise and at their lowest at about 11:00 P.M.
(*"Parade Hotline," Parade Magazine, 6/29/80, p. 24; Mitchell, p. 11*)

Hormone Production During Middle Age
Men: Hormonal production declines only 1 percent per year. By the time a man is seventy-five years old, his hormonal production is about that of a ten-year-old boy.
Women: In the first year or two of menopause, a woman's production of estrogen is reduced to about one fourth of her menstrual level.
(*Wagenvoord/Bailey, Men, p. 154*)

Hormone Production in Embryos
Males: By the sixth week of development, the human male embryo is producing male hormones.
Females: Not until the twelfth week of development does the female embryo begin producing ovarian hormones.,
(*Wagenvoord/Bailey, Men, p. 22*)

Hormones, Sex
Hormones are chemical messengers that deliver information to the cells indicating how tall you will grow, when you ovulate if you are a female, how much energy you have, when you want to make love, or how well you digest your food. The sex hormones are those that are related to our sexual functions. The most prominent are estrogens (the female hormones), and androgens (the male hormones, including testosterone, progesterone, folli-

cle-stimulating hormone, and the luteinizing hormone). All these hormones are present in both sexes but the quantities differ considerably from person to person and from day to day, making comparisons difficult. For instance, a woman can produce from one half as much to ten times as much estrogen as a man, depending upon which phase of the menstrual cycle she is in, and she can produce anywhere from fifty to two hundred fifty times as much progesterone as a man. A man produces from ten to fifteen times as much testosterone as a woman.

(*Behrman and Vaughn, pp. 1837, 1846; Mitchell, p. 12; Money, p. 207; Eastman, p. 95*)

Household Workers
Only 2 percent of all the household workers in the U.S.A. are men.

(*Bird, p. 119*)

House of Representatives
In 1983 only 22 of the 435 members of the House of Representatives were female.

(*Scott, p. 2*)

House of Representatives, History of Elections
Since 1776, there have been 9,591 representatives elected to the House. Of those, only 87 have been women.

(*Bird, p. 107*)

Housework
According to one study, men spend an average of one hour and seven minutes a day, while women spend six hours and forty-eight minutes a day, on housework.

(*Brothers*, Woman's Day, *1/12/82, p. 48*)

Another set of statistics indicates that women spend twenty-six hours per week and men only thirty-six minutes per week on housework.

(*Pogrebin, p. 144*)

Professional men are more likely than nonprofessional men to help with the housework.

(*McCall's*, February 1983, p. 76)

Housework, Boring
As many women as men find housework boring.
(McCall's, February 1983, p. 76)

Hugging
Little girls get more face-to-face hugs than little boys.
(Serbin and O'Leary, p. 102)

Humanitarian
Women are believed to be more humanitarian than men.
(Rubin, Psychology Today, November 1982, p. 12)

Humanities and the Arts
Male: In the academic year 1979–80, 60.4 percent of the doctorate degrees in the humanities and the arts were awarded to men.
Female: 39.6 percent were awarded to women.
(Hacker, p. 244)

Husband-Wife Murders
The FBI estimates that about 12.5 percent of all murders in the U.S.A. are husband-wife killings.
(Bird, p. 91)

Hyperactive
Ninety-five percent of those classified as hyperactive are male. There are an estimated two million hyperactive males in the United States.
(Gottlieb, p. 82)

Hypercholesterolemia
(A family tendency to accumulate cholesterol)
Female: In women with hypercholesterolemia, the risk of developing heart disease is greater than for the average female, but is still lower than the risk to the average man.
Male: If a man inherits a tendency to accumulate cholesterol, he will be at greater risk of developing heart disease by the time he is fifty-five than will other men of the same age.
(Health, January 1982, p. 22)

Hypertension
High blood pressure, also known as hypertension, affects 34 million Americans. After menopause, a woman's chances of becoming hypertensive increase.

(Dustan [unnumbered pages])

Hypochondria
A hypochondriac believes she or he has some terrible disease in spite of the fact that there is no evidence to support the belief. The majority of sufferers who live in great fear of their imagined diseases are women.

(Cooley, p. 286)

Hysteric
More females than males are classified as hysteric.

(Kolb, p. 91)

I

Ideal Man, What the Sexes Want
Male: Most men feel the ideal man would be warm and loving.
Female: Women feel the ideal man would be gentle, expressive,
and romantic.
(*Tavris, p. 35;* Psychology Today, *January 1977*)

Ideal Woman, What the Sexes Want
Males: The man's ideal is a woman who has developed a comfortable balance between her family and self-realization.
Females: Women think men want a woman who is passive and submissive and always chooses her family over any outside interest.
(Women in Therapy, *Franks and Burtle, editors, pp. 58, 59*)

Illness, Days in Bed
Males: The average man spends 5.6 days a year in bed.
Females: The average woman spends 7.8 days a year ill in bed.
(Census Abstract, *p. 115*)

Illness, Rate
While the illness rate is higher for females, they are more likely
than males to recover.
(Census, *p. 115;* Science Digest, *September 1982, p. 90*)

Illnesses, Minor
Women report more minor illnesses than men.
(*Rubinstein, p. 32*)

Immune Globulin M
(A protein that helps the body resist disease.)

Women have more M than men. The presence of estrogen is thought to be a related factor, as estrogen injected into animals activates the production of M.

(*Dranov*, p. 32)

Immunity
The female's immunity system is stronger than the male's due to the extra protection of the genes in the X chromosomes against infection, as well as to the higher levels of globulin M.

Men are more susceptible to disease due to the fact that they have only one X chromosome, whereas women have two X chromosomes. The X chromosome carries immunity genes and, as women have two, they have a backup. If one is not adequate, the other will take over.

(Science Digest, *September 1982*, p. 90)

Inanimate Objects, Response to
Males: Infant boys will respond positively and with interest to an inanimate object such as a toy as easily as to a person.
Females: Infant girls respond more to a person than to an object, preferring interaction with a human being to playing with a toy. (This preference seems to continue into adulthood.)

(Newsweek, *5/18/81*, p. 73)

Incest
Boys: It is estimated that about 10 percent of boys have a sexual encounter with an adult—usually a relative.
Girls: Between one fourth and one third of all girls are approached sexually by an adult male. Ten percent have a sexual encounter with a relative.

(*Harmon*, Harvard Medical School Healthletter, *March 1981*, p. 3)

Income
Men receive 70 percent of the income in the United States.

(*Jencks*, p. 73)

Income, Family
More than 85 percent of the men bring home the majority of the
family income.
  (Lingeman, p. 10)

Income, Median, of Full-time Employed Workers (includes income from employment as well as from other sources)
Male: In 1980 the median income for men was $19,173.
Female: The median income for women was $11,591. (The me-
dian income for women workers is 60 percent of men's.)
  (Hacker. p. 149)

Income, Supplemental Security
The majority of the 4.2 million people who receive this benefit
are women who are aged, blind, or disabled.
  (Ehrenreich and Stallard, p. 221)

Income after Five or More Years (among persons 25 years or older)
Male: The median income of men who have worked five years or
more is $22,800.
Female: The median income of women who have worked five
years or more is $11,900.
  (U.S.A. Statistics in Brief, p. 145)

Income and Sex

Income	Male	Female
Over $75,000	442,000	12,000
$50,000–75,000	1,103,000	37,000
$20,000–25,000	7,550,000	1,414,000
$10,000–15,000	8,366,000	8,089,000
$ 5,000–10,000	4,574,000	7,612,000
Under $5,000	1,495,000	1,276,000
  (Hacker, p. 148)

Income of Persons 25 Years Old
Male: In 1980, the median income of men twenty-five years old
was $19,100.
Female: The median income of twenty-five-year-old women was
$8,100.
  (U.S.A. Statistics in Brief, p. 145)

Industry and Discrimination Against Women
Women in industry with identical educations and work experience as men can expect to earn less, and have less expectation of advancement.
(Kantel, pp. 10–13)

Infant Care
Males: Men play with infants more than women do. The father tends to relate to the baby more when the mother is not present.
(Mitchell, p. 80)
Females: "In all human societies, females do most of the infant care." Women assume more of a caretaking role than men do, holding and cuddling the baby, and respond more to infant faces than men do. Females tend to leave infant males alone to explore on their own, while interfering more often in activities of infant girl babies.
(Mitchell, pp. 80, 86, 87)

Infant Differences
Boys are awake more than girls are. They also display more facial grimacing and engage in more movement.
(Newsweek, 5/18/81, p. 73)

Infertility, Causes of
Males: As far as we know, the causes of male infertility are impotence, and poor quality and quantity of the sperm in the ejaculation. Problems relating to low sperm count can be due to heat, stress, poor health, prolonged sexual abstinence, genital abnormality, childhood or adulthood diseases, and exposure to X rays or certain chemicals.
(Cooke and Dworkin, p. 98)
Females: The causes of infertility in the female include a failure to ovulate due to hormonal imbalance (this is seen as the major cause), genital fluids that may be inadequate to transport sperm, genital abnormality (such as a divided uterus), or previous infections causing blockage of the fallopian tubes.
(Cooke and Dworkin, p. 98)

Infertility, Statistics Relating to
Ten percent of the population who want children cannot have them.

Men: In 30 percent to 35 percent of the cases, the problem is due to the male.
Women: In 50 percent to 55 percent of the cases, the problem is due to the female.

It is the problem of both partners in about 15 percent of the cases.

(Woman's Body, p. 160)

Influenza
Males are more likely than females to suffer from influenza.

(Brothers, Woman's Day, 2/9/82, p. 138)

Injuries
Male: 38.1 million men were injured in 1979.
Female: 29.4 million women were injured in 1979.

(Census, p. 115)

Men and women are equally likely to be injured at home.
Males: Men outnumber women in the number of accidents, and are six times more likely to be injured at work.
Females: Women are the victims of only 37 out of 100 accidents that occur at work.

(Almanac, 1980, p. 140)

Injuries in Sports, Frequencies and Location of
(The female is much better balanced due to her lower center of gravity, so, biologically, her chances of having an injury are fewer than a man's. However, his greater experience in sports, and the cultural expectation that he will be athletic, give him an equal edge.)

The frequency of sports injuries in females is lower than in males. Males have more serious injuries, and when females do have injuries they are usually sprains or strains in the lower extremities. Women are more prone to knee problems (see "Runner's Knee") due to the manner in which her knee joint is attached to her thigh and calf.

(Klafs and Arnheim, p. 184)

Injury Rate Among College Athletes
Male: Male college athletes report more severe genitalia injuries than do females, whose reproductive organs are internal and therefore more secure.

Female: Female college athletes report a higher rate of "over-strain" than do male college athletes. Such conditions as bursae tenderness are reported four times as often among college female athletes as among male athletes.

    (Klafs and Arnheim, p. 191)

Insomnia

Two times as many women have trouble falling asleep.

    (Willis, p. 37)

Insurance Rates and Discrimination

Rates are higher for women on individual health insurance plans than they are for men.

    (Ms., February 1983, p. 83)

Intelligence

There are no discernible differences between the sexes in the results of most intelligence tests.

    (Fryer, p. 242)

Intelligence and Accomplishment

Males: There is a close relationship between IQ and accomplishment in men.

Females: There is no relationship between IQ and accomplishment in women. (Dowling cites research that traced people with high IQ scores from childhood to adulthood. The results are astonishing: two thirds of the women who had genius level IQs of 170 or above were housewives or office workers. The men with high IQs were achievers.)

    (Dowling, p. 32)

Intelligence Tests and Noise Levels

Boys do better than girls when tests are conducted in noisy rooms. Girls do better than boys in quiet rooms.

    (Cory, April 1982, p. 20)

Intimacy, Value of

Male: Most men discover the value of intimacy, relationships, and care at midlife.

Female: Women appreciate these qualities for years prior to mid-life.
(*Gilligan, pp. 68–71*)

Intuition
Women are much more likely to be able to interpret correctly the meaning behind a person's facial expression, body movement, and tone of voice than men are. (Studies relating to the subject have been conducted time and time again since 1920 with similar results.)

Neuropsychologist Deborah Weber speculates that this is because the two sides of a woman's brain are more closely connected (see brain differences) than a man's, and can transmit information back and forth more rapidly than a man can.
(*Hammer, p. 26; Eppingham, p. 37*)

Involutional Depression
Males: Men may develop involutional depression around the ages of sixty to sixty-five. Symptoms in a man include feelings of apathy, failure, and hopelessness, loss of sexual interest, or a feeling that his family does not love him.
Females: This kind of chronic depression is more common in women than in men. It occurs most frequently at about age forty-five to fifty, following stresses such as a death in the family or menopause. Complaints include sleeplessness, crying spells, and feelings of worthlessness and failure.
(*Cooley, p. 292*)

Involutional Psychotic Reaction, Depressive Types
The incidence of involutional psychotic reaction is two to three times greater in women than in men.
(*Kolb, p. 358*)

Iron
Females need twice as much iron as men.
(*Selden, p. 52*)

Jail Confinement
Male: In 1978, 148,839, or 94 percent, of those confined to local jails were men.
Female: 9,555, or 6 percent, of those confined were women.
(Hacker, p. 231)

Jealousy
(The following four entries on jealousy were compiled from research conducted by Eliot Aronson, University of California at Santa Cruz, and Ayala Pines, University of California at Berkeley.)
   Neither sex is more jealous than the other.

Jealousy, Breaking Up Because of
Men are more likely to break up with a woman who makes them jealous than vice versa.

Jealousy, Reaction to
Males: In reacting to jealousy, men usually seek to repair their injured self-esteem.
Females: Women seek to repair the relationship itself.

Jealousy, Response to
Male: Men are inclined to turn jealous anger inward, confront the woman with it, or seek revenge.
Female: Women are more likely to respond with feelings of help-

lessness, betrayal, insecurity, and inadequacy, and tend to seek the support of a friend, make plans to get even, and to cry when alone.

(*Coping with Jealousy, Social Behavior*, Human Behavior, *November 1978, p. 12*)

Jealousy, the Way It Feels
Men feel less physical and emotional pain as a result of jealousy than women do.

(*Adams*, Psychology Today, *p. 38*)

Jealousy, Who Has It?
Jealousy is most likely to occur in people with low self-esteem and feelings of inadequacy, and in those who want a relationship to be rather exclusive.

Male: The male who becomes jealous is usually one who feels that males should have more sexual freedom than females.

Female: Jealousy is likely to appear in a woman who places a relationship in a position of great importance, outweighing any other part of her life.

Job, Love on the
A female is twice as likely as a male to be fired if trouble ensues as a result of an interoffice affair, due to complaints of favoritism from co-workers.

(*Researcher: Robert Quinn, Ph.D.*, Human Behavior, *February 1978, p. 59*)

Job Changes
Each month 2.2 percent of all males and 2.6 percent of all females change their jobs.

(*Wagenvoord/Bailey*, Women, *p. 27*)

Job Hours Worked
Both males and females work an average of 39.7 hours per week.

(*Department of Labor*)

Job Loss During a Recession
In a recession females in service, sales, or clerical jobs hold onto their jobs longer than men do.

(Psychology Today, *December 1981, p. 19; Researcher: Daniel Cornfield, Vanderbilt University*)

Job Satisfaction
Most Americans, both male and female, are satisfied with their jobs, especially those whose yearly income is over $25,000. (Only 13 percent of those making less than $5,000 a year were satisfied.)
(Thatcher, November 1978, p. 12)

Job-Sharing
(When two or more people share a 40-hour-a-week job and its salary.)
More women than men job-share.
(Nollen, p. 153)

Job Stress
Women are subjected to more job-related stress than men, and are able to cope with it better. (Some authorities feel this is due to the fact it is considered more acceptable for women than for men to vent their feelings.)
(Human Behavior, January 1979, p. 34)

Joints
A woman's joints are more flexible and less tightly hinged than a man's.
(Signe Hammer, p. 20)

Jokes
Male: Men like sexual, ethnic, and word-play jokes more than women do.
Female: Women like silly and absurd jokes better than men do.
Both like hostile jokes equally.
(Hassett and Houlihan, p. 64)
Women are very sensitive about their bodies, so no one should ever joke about them! A man can take teasing about his figure; a woman can't!
(Ford, p. 111)

Judges, Appellate and Trial Court
Male: In 1977, 5,830 men were judges.
Female: 110 women were judges.
(Bird, p. 112)

Judges, Federal
Male: There are 627 male federal judges.
Female: There are 48 female federal judges.
   (Field, p. 78)

Jumping
Men can jump farther and can take longer strides than women because they have longer legs and have more acceleration due to greater muscular strength.
   (Dyer, p. 109; Man's Body, pp. A13–15)

Jury Duty
Both sexes are equally eligible for jury duty.
   (Ross and Barcher, p. 211)
The foreman (leader of the jury) is almost always a man.
   (Mitchell, p. 114)

Keypunch Operators
95.9 percent of keypunch operators are female.
(Hacker, p. 128)

Kidney Damage as a Result of Diabetes
More men than women suffer kidney damage as a result of diabetes.
(Brothers, Woman's Day, 2/9/82, p. 138)

Kidney Disorders
Disorders of the kidney are more common in women than in men. Many feel this is due to the close proximity of the female's anus and ureter, which permits more bacterial entry.
(Woman's Body, p. 366)

Klinefelter's Syndrome
(A condition in which, due to an imbalance in hormonal secretions, there is a delay in physical maturation.)
   Klinefelter's syndrome occurs in males only, and there is a mental defect found in one fourth of those afflicted. Boys or men with Klinefelter's syndrome are usually tall, lean, with breast enlargement and small or undeveloped testes, and limited sex drive.
(Kolb, p. 581)

Knee Problems in Adolescence
(The knee is the largest and one of the most complex joints in the

body. It is also one of the most vulnerable to injury or trauma.) *Males:* A bump below the kneecap, often painful and inflamed, is caused by bone changes during rapid growth. This condition is called Osgood-Schlatter disease.

Females: A girl who is knock-kneed may later develop a dislocating kneecap, common in young women.

(Knee Owner's Manual, *pp. 3, 10*)

Knock-Knees

More women than men are knock-kneed.

(Good Looks, *December 1981, p. 20*)

Labor Force
Males: 62 million men in the United States are employed.
Females: 47.3 million women (51 percent of the female population) in the United States are employed.
(There are about 230 million people in the United States.)
(Time, *7/12/82, p. 23*)

Labor Force, Percentage of Male and Female Between the Ages of 18 and 64
Males: Fifty percent to 53.3 percent of the labor force is between the ages of eighteen and sixty-four and male.
Females: Forty percent to 42 percent is between the ages of eighteen and sixty-four and female.
(*Bird, p. 112*)

Labor Force, Years in
Males: The average working male spends forty-three years in the labor force.
Females: The average single working female averages forty-five years in the working force.
(*Wagenvoord/Bailey*, Women, *p. 279*)

Labor Force and Marital Status
Male: 81 percent of married men are in the labor force.
Female: 50.2 percent of married women are in the labor force.
(45 percent of those women have children under six.)
(U.S.A. Statistics in Brief, *p. 144*)

Labor-Union Membership
In 1980 there were 20,095,000 Americans who belonged to a labor union.
Male: 28.4 percent of all employed men were union members.
Female: 15.9 percent of all employed women belonged to a union.
(Hacker, p. 137)

Language Disorders
Males are more likely than females to have language disorders.
(Arkoff, p. 64)
Stuttering is three times more prevalent in males than in females, and five times as many boys as girls have difficulty learning to talk.
(Durden-Smith, p. 52)

Languages, Doctorates in
Male: 227 males received doctorates in languages in 1980.
Female: 303 females received doctorates in languages that year.
(U.S. Statistical Abstract, p. 166)

Languages, Foreign
Females learn foreign languages more easily than men do.
("Ideas," Newsweek, 5/18/81, p. 72)

Languages, Master's Degrees
Male: 667 master's degrees in languages were awarded to men in 1980.
Female: 1,590 master's degrees in languages were awarded to women that year.
(U.S. Statistics, p. 166)

Law Degrees
Male: 69.8 percent of the law degrees awarded in the 1979–80 academic year went to men.
Female: 30.2 percent were awarded to women.
(Hacker, p. 244)

Law School Students

In the 1979–80 academic year, 33.5 percent of law school students were female, in contrast to 3.6 percent in 1963.
(Murphy, p. 51)

Law Violators and the Marital State

Male: More single men than married men are law violators.
Female: More married women than single women are law violators.
(Bernard, p. 30)

Leadership

When a group is made up of both sexes, it is likely that the leader chosen will be male. In a study undertaken in 1976, it was found that when women fail as leaders, it is not held against them as much as it is against men, as "they are not supposed to be good leaders anyway."
(Parlee, p. 65; Mitchell, p. 114)
In a 1976 study by Bartol and Wortman, the style of female leaders was seen to differ from that of men in that women are less authoritarian, show more consideration, and show more satisfaction with co-workers than male leaders do.
(Mitchell, p. 116)

Learning Disabled

Male: Eighty percent of those who are learning disabled are male.
Female: Twenty percent are female.
(Farnham-Diggory, p. 36)

Left-handedness

More men than women are left-handed.
(News of Medicine, p. 31)

Left-Hemisphere Brain Development

The left hemisphere, the side of the brain where language is organized, develops more slowly in males than in females (some feel this is why females excel in verbal activities until high school, when males catch up).
(Durden-Smith, p. 53)

Legionnaire's Disease
Three times as many men as women succumb to Legionnaire's Disease.

(Brothers, Woman's Day, 2/9/82, p. 138)

Legislators, State, 1983
In 1983 women held 13 percent of the legislative seats in state governments, with a total of 991 seats.

(Honolulu Advertiser, *12/5/83, p. F2*)

Legs
Women have more fatty tissue on their legs than men, probably due to the activity of estrogen. A woman's legs tend to be soft due to the extra fat; a man's are more sinewy.

(Duff, p. 86)

Legs and Running
Men's legs are bigger and stronger than women's, enabling them to run faster.

(Selden, p. 53)

Leg Wrestling
A woman can be as strong in the leg muscles as a man of the same weight, and she can compete equally, if trained, in leg wrestling. A woman's wide pelvic area also gives her additional leverage, which is an advantage in leg wrestling.

(Hammer, p. 21)

Leukemia
More men than women die from leukemia.

(Brothers, Woman's Day, 2/9/82, p. 138)

Library Assistants
77.4 percent of library assistants are female.

(Hacker, p. 128)

Life Expectancy
Male: The life expectancy for men born in 1980 is 68.8 years.
Female: The life expectancy for women born in 1980 is 77.5 years.

(U.S.A. Statistics in Brief, *p. 145)*

The average American male lives to be 69.3 and the female to be 77.1
  (*Murphy, p. 50*)

Life Expectancy and Marital Status
Males: Single males have the shortest life expectancy of all categories.
Females: Single females have the highest life expectancy of all categories.
  (*"Let's Put Our Heads Together," p. 22*)

Light, Sensitivity to
Females are more sensitive to light than males are, beginning in infancy.
  (*Gottlieb, p. 82*)

Liver at Birth
The liver of a female infant is heavier than that of a male infant. All other major organs are heavier in the male.
  (Man's Body, pp. A05–06)

Living to Age 500
Seventy-nine percent of the men who answered one survey indicated that they would like to live to be 500. Only 50 percent of the women polled indicated they would like to live to be 500. The author of the survey felt that women "view life as a losing battle," whereas men view it as "a challenge to be overcome."
  (*Rubinstein,* Psychology Today, *March 1983, p. 81*)

Loneliness and Old Age
In a Harris Poll in 1976, older women spoke of loneliness twice as much as older men did.
  (*Bird, p. 155*)

Long-distance Running
Men can run faster than women, but women can endure running longer as they have about 10 percent more fat on their bodies.
  (*Selden, p. 96*)
The primary fuel utilized in aerobic exercise is glycogen (sugar stored in the liver and released for energy), but fatty tissue has

an energy yield seven times higher than that of glycogen. The human heart muscle uses fat tissue in preference to glycogen in prolonged exercise (as do the hearts of many species, such as birds, during migration). So a woman's extra fat gives her an advantage in long-distance running.

(*Dyer, p. 110*)

Longevity

Women live an average of eight years longer than men.

(*Horn, p. 20*)

By age sixty-five, there are only seven men to every ten women. Over sixty-five, there are one hundred men to every one hundred fifty women.

(Man's Body, pp. A31–32)

Longevity, Determining Factors Among Those over 60 Years Old

Among people of sixty years or older, those who are satisfied with their work, whether it is paid or unpaid, are likely to live longest (in the cases of both men and women).

(*Crocket, p. 11*)

Some of the reasons women live longer than men are:

(a) They have two times as many disease-fighting genes as men, giving them protection against infections and cancers.

(b) Their life-styles are not as destructive as men's.

(c) They have more of the M protein, which has protective qualities.

(d) They have much smaller hearts, so their heart muscles do not have to work as hard as men's.

(e) They can adapt better physically.

(f) They see physicians twice as often as men do so the likelihood of diagnosing a disease early, which prevents its progression, is greater.

(g) They have protection from high levels of estrogen and low levels of testosterone.

(*Interview, Irving Marvit, M.D., 1983*)

Longevity and Blood Type

Males: Men with type O blood tend to live longer lives than do men with type B blood.

Females: Females with type *B* blood tend to live longer than females with type *O*.

(Science Digest, *January 1984, p. 82*)

Loss, Reaction to

More women than men respond to loss with depression. Widowers have a higher death and suicide rate than widows, however, though widows have a higher cancer rate than single or married women.

(Modern Maturity, *12/81–1/82, p. 12*)

Loud Volumes

At eighty-five decibels and above, any sound seems twice as loud to women as it does to men.

(Goleman, *p. 59*)

Love Addicts

Love addicts need love desperately, but are also desperately afraid of it. There are more female than male love addicts. (The females tend to fall in love with unattainable or totally inappropriate men who will hurt them.)

(Krentz, *p. C9*)

Lunch, School

Forty-eight percent of families who utilize the school lunch program are headed by women.

(Ehrenreich and Stallard, *p. 221*)

Lungs, Adult

A male adult's lungs can hold two quarts more air than a woman's.

(Selden, *July 1981, p. 53*)

Lungs at Birth

Male lungs are larger than female lungs at birth.

(Man's Body, *pp. A05–06*)

Lupus, Systemic

(A disease that affects approximately 500,000 people and usually occurs between the ages of twenty and forty. The disease is characterized by a red rash which appears on the face [the word *lupus* means wolf in Latin as the rash is said to make one resemble a wolf]. Other symptoms are fever, arthritis, anemia, kidney disfunction, and gastrointestinal inflammation. Stress can bring on or aggravate the disease.)

Ten times as many women as men (a total of over 450,000 women) have lupus.

(Science Digest, *September 1982, p. 90*)

Luteinizing Hormone
This hormone, found in males and females, stimulates ovulation and the formation of the corpus luteum, a yellow mass in the ovary that produces progesterone (the pregnancy hormone) in women. It is called the ICSH in males (or the interstitial cell) and stimulates the production of testosterone and other male hormones.

(Mitchell, *p. 11;* Grollman, *pp. 572–575*)

Lymphoma
More men than women die from this type of cancer.

(Brothers, *Woman's Day, 2/9/82, p. 138*)

Maids and Servants
95.9 percent of maids and servants are female.
(Hacker, p. 127)

Majors
In 1980, of 49,194 majors in the armed services, only 2,172 were female.
(Hacker, p. 206)

Male/Female Ratio at Various Ages
At age 20: There are equal numbers of men and women.
At age 30: There are more women than men.
At age 65: For every ten women, there are only seven men.
(Man's Body, pp. A31–32; Mitchell, p. 167)

Male Sex Hormones
Males: Male sex hormones, called androgens, are mainly produced in the testes, but are also produced by the adrenal glands (glands located above the kidney). Testosterone is the most potent of the androgens.
Females: Women produce androgens, in small amounts, in the ovaries and the adrenals.
(Money, p. 210; Mitchell, p. 39)

Managers, Corporate
Six percent of corporate managers are women.
(Porter, p. 22)

Managers and Administrators
In 1983, 28 percent of managers and administrators were women.
(D. Rubin, p. 59)

Managers and Commitment to Work
The number of female managers has doubled in the last ten years, yet the roster of the American Managers' Association remains male-dominated by a ratio of 9 to 1. A recent study reveals the following regarding differences in male and female managers: women are more likely than men to make sacrifices for their jobs; they are more career-oriented and get more satisfaction from their jobs than men; more women than men would forgo an important function at home if it conflicted with the job. More women than men said they would accept a job that would significantly change their life-style.
(Bridgewater, p. 17)

Manic Depressive Psychotic Reaction
(This severe illness usually sets in during the ages of twenty to thirty. Victims of either sex are afflicted with severe depression and equally emotionally charged "highs" when overstimulated and overexcited.)
    This condition occurs about twice as frequently in women as in men and the average onset in women is earlier than it is in men.
(Kolb, p. 367)

Manual Dexterity
Females excel in fine motor coordination and score higher than men on tests involving speed and accuracy, such as in typing. As females do display "superior tactile sensitivity" (McGuinness's term), women are generally better at such things as typing, needlework, and neurosurgery.
(Goleman, p. 59; Gelman in Newsweek, 5/18/81, p. 73)

MAO Activity
MAO, monoamine oxidase, is an enzyme that has been associated with depression, and some researchers feel it is a key to why women get depressed prior to and during menstruation.

This enzyme rises during the premenstrual phase. During the rest of the cycle it is lower than it is in normal males (even at its peak it is no higher than it normally is in males).

(Eastman, p. 95)

Marijuana

Male: Nineteen percent of the men in this country are marijuana users.

Female: Fourteen percent of the women in the U.S.A. use marijuana.

(U.S. Institute on Drug Abuse, National Survey, 1979; U.S.A. Statistical Abstract, 1980, p. 122)

Marijuana and Hormonal Disruption

Male: Heavy usage has been shown to cause a reduction in sperm count, a reduction of well-shaped sperm, and breast enlargement in some males. Apparently the system returns to normal a short time after drug use ceases. Some authorities are concerned that heavy usage in prepubescent or pubescent boys might interfere with the development of the reproductive glands.

(Angier, p. 77)

Female: Heavy use of this drug is more disruptive to the female hormonal system than it is to that of the male. The female system is more complicated, and heavy usage can cause a disruption in the menstrual cycle and cessation of ovulation and menses.

(Angier, p. 77)

Marine Enlisted Personnel

3.7 percent of Marine enlisted personnel are female.

(Hacker, p. 207)

Marine Officers

2.7 percent of Marine officers are female.

(Hacker, p. 207)

Marital Status, Distribution in 1981

Male: Single (never been married): 23.9 percent of the population

Married: 67.8 percent

Widowed (and single): 2.5 percent

Divorced (and single): 5.7 percent
Female: Single (never been married): 17.4 percent
Married: 62.4 percent
Widowed (and single): 12.01 percent
Divorced (and single): 7.6 percent
(Statistical Abstract of the U.S., p. 39)

Marital Status, Divorced
In 1981, for every 1,000 divorced women, there were 666 divorced men.
(Hacker, p. 101)

Marital Status, Separated
In 1981, for every 1,000 separated women there were 668 separated men.
(Hacker, p. 101)

Marital Status, Widowed
In 1981, for every 1,000 widows, there were 188 widowers.
(Hacker, p. 101)

Marriage, First, Median Age of
Males: The median age at which men marry for the first time is 24.8.
Females: The median age for women is 22.3.
(Sanoff, p. 53)

Marriage, Source of Problems in
In most cases, both husband and wife believe it is the husband who causes the problems in a marriage.
(Bernard, p. 31)

Marriage and Age
Men marry women who are an average of 2.3 years younger than they are.
(Sanoff, p. 53)

Marriage and Criminal Behavior
Men: More single men than married men commit crimes.
(Bernard, p. 18)

Women: More married than single women commit crimes. (Marriage does not protect women as it does men.)
(*Bernard, p. 32*)

Marriage and Happiness
Men: Numerous studies report that marriage is good for men and makes them happy. Almost twice as many married men as singles report being happy.
Women: Married females report greater unhappiness than single women do with or without children.
(*Brothers, Woman's Day, 1/12/82, p. 44*)

Marriage and Illness
Men: Married men experience less illness and live longer than single men.
Women: Married women are emotionally and physically ill more often and die sooner than women who remain single.
(New Woman, *11/12/79, p. 10*)

Marriage and Morality
Married males and females show a greater sense of social conformity and morality than do the unmarried.
(*Bernard, pp. 16–27*)

Marriage Counseling
Eight out of ten appointments to see marriage counselors are made by men. (In 1968, one out of ten husbands sought marriage counseling.)
(*Star, p. 33 [From a study by Dr. Ray Fowler]*)

Master's Degree Programs
In the 1982–83 academic year, equal numbers of men and women were enrolled in master's degree programs.
(*Murphy, p. 50*)

Masturbation and Age
Male: Ninety-three percent of men masturbate and do so throughout their lives.
Female: By the age of forty-five, 62 percent of all women have

masturbated. Masturbation is common among older women.
(Man's Body, *p. 32;* Woman's Body, *p. 44; Mitchell, p. 167)*

Masturbation and Fantasy

Male: About half of the men surveyed usually fantasize during masturbation.
Female: More than half of the females indicate that they fantasize during masturbation.
(Woman's Body, *p. 48)*

Math, Doctorates

In the 1979–80 academic year, 12.8 percent of the Ph.D.s in math were awarded to women.
(Hacker, *p. 244)*

Math Ability

Males are superior to females in mathematical aptitude at puberty, and this continues into adulthood. Studies on sexual differences in math ability are frequent and famous. Most say that men excel in math, especially in geometry and trigonometry.
(Benlow and Stanley in Science *Magazine, 12/12/80)*

Math and Physical Sciences, Ph.D.

Male: In 1982, 88 percent of all Ph.D.s in math and physical sciences were awarded to men.
Female: Twelve percent went to women.
(Yalow, *p. 23)*

Math and Verbal Skills, Equality in and Age

When children are nine years old, they score equally in math and verbal skills. Boys go on to excel in math, and girls to excel at verbal skills.
(Bird, *p. 106; National Assessment for Educational Progress)*

Math Scores

Four times as many boys, age twelve and thirteen, receive high grades on the math sections of aptitude tests as do girls of the same age. Julian Stanley and Camilla Benbow noted in Science *Magazine* that mathematically gifted males may have been exposed to unusually high amounts of testosterone in the womb.

(*Global Report*, Honolulu Advertiser, *11/28/83*)

Maturation, Physical

Women mature physically faster than men.

(Newsweek, *5/18/81, p. 78*)

Boys: A growth spurt begins at the age of about thirteen and a half and continues for six years.

Girls: A growth spurt peaks at about age twelve and tapers off by fourteen or fifteen.

(Woman's Body, *p. 416*)

Mazes

Maze tests given within IQ tests indicate that males are better than females at maze readings.

(Goleman, *p. 49*)

Mechanical Tasks

Men are believed to excel at mechanical tasks because their perceptions of depth and space are superior to women's.

(Newsweek, *5/18/81, p. 73*)

Media Jobs

Males: In 1977, men held 65 to 75 percent of the jobs in the media field.

Females: Women held 25 to 35 percent of the jobs in the media field.

(Bird, *p. 141*)

Medicaid

Male: In 1982, 39 percent of those who utilized Medicaid were male.

Female: Sixty-one percent of Medicaid recipients were female.

(Ehrenreich and Stallard, *p. 221*)

Medical School Graduates

Male: In the 1979–80 academic year, 89 percent of medical school graduates were men.

Female: 11 percent were women.

(Census, *p. 151*)

Medical School Students
Male: In the 1982–83 academic year, 74 percent of the medical students were men.
Female: Twenty-six percent of medical students were women.
(Caudle, p. 8)

Medicare
Male: In 1982, 40 percent of those enrolled in Medicare were male.
Female: Sixty percent of those enrolled in Medicare were female.
(Ehrenreich and Stallard, p. 221)

Medication
Women take 50 percent to 80 percent more medication than men.
(Verbrugge, Parade Magazine, 11/14/82)

Medroxyprogesterone
Provera or Depo-Provera is the market name for this pharmaceutical hormonal product. It is utilized therapeutically as a means of birth control, suppressing ovulation in women and preventing the formation of sperm in men. It is also used to suppress the release of male hormones in male sex offenders.
(Money, p. 219)

Memory
Women are believed to have better memories than men, especially for people they have not seen for a long time.
(Psychology Today, November 1978, p. 59)

Memory Recall
Women excel at memory recall.
(Newsweek, 5/18/81, p. 73)

Mental Breakdown, Reports of
Women report more symptoms of mental breakdown than men do.
(Bernard, p. 130)

Mental Health of the Unmarried
Among people who have never been married, about twice as many males as females have mental health problems.
(Bernard, pp. 28–59)

Mental Health Services, Use of
Women utilize mental health services twice as much as men do.
(Bird, p. 125)

Mental Hospitals, Admission to
More males than females are admitted to mental hospitals.
(Franks and Burtle, p. 370)

Mental Hospitals, First Admission Under Age 15
Twice as many boys as girls are first admissions to public mental hospitals.
(Sexton, p. 74)

Mental Illness
There is a higher incidence of mental illness among women than among men.
(Bernard, p. 31)

Mental Retardation
More men than women are mentally retarded.
(Health, p. 23)

Metabolic Rate
The average woman's metabolic rate is 6 percent to 10 percent lower than that of a male of comparable size.
(Klafs and Arnheim, p. 184)

Metabolic Rate and Calories
Men burn 39.5 calories per square meter of body surface, whereas women burn only 37 calories per square meter of body surface.
(Cooke and Dworkin, p. 53)

Midlife Crisis
Midlife crisis is usually defined as a time of questioning: Have I

done what I should have done? What have I missed? Did I make the right decisions? What should I do with the rest of my life? Both men and women experience midlife crisis.

(Levinson, p. 73; Interview in U.S. News & World Report, 10/25/82)

Migraine Headache

More women than men are afflicted by this painful headache. Reports indicate that 12 to 15 million people are afflicted, and that three fourths of those are female.

("Right Now," McCall's, August 1982, p. 46)

Militance

Women are thought to be less militant than men.

(Rubin, Psychology Today, November 1982, p. 13)

Military Personnel

8.4 percent of all military personnel are female.

(Hacker, p. 207)

Mineral Needs

Males: Men need more of the mineral selenium, less iron, and slightly more magnesium than women need.

Females: The primary deficiency among women who menstruate, or are pregnant or nursing, is iron. They usually get about half of what they need. After menopause, the need for calcium increases greatly, and the need for iron decreases.

(Stump, p. 137)

Miscarriage

The majority of fetuses lost in miscarriages are males.

(Brothers, p. 16)

Mitral Valve Prolapse

This is a harmless but frightening heart condition that affects from 5 percent to 10 percent of young women but seldom occurs in men. If there are symptoms, the woman may feel jittery or dizzy with her heart pounding in a frightening manner. Apparently the cause is related to a sensitivity to adrenaline and other hormones.

(Oppenheim, p. 24)

Money, Meaning of
Male: Money seems to represent identity and power to men.
Female: To a woman, money represents security and autonomy.
(Research by Blumstein and Schwartz in Ms., p. 116)

Money, Telling What You Have
Women are more likely to reveal their financial situation than
men are.
(Rubinstein, p. 34, 5/81)

Monogamy
Both men and women believe in monogamy, according to
Schwartz and Blumstein. Heterosexual men are slightly more
monogamous than heterosexual women.
(Ms., p. 116)

Mood Changes
Males: There is some evidence that men's moods change every
four to nine weeks as a result of hormonal changes. Some men
have testosterone cycles ranging from eight to thirty days. Men
report mood changes ranging from depression, apathy, and with-
drawal, to feelings of well being.
Females: Many women report a sense of well being at the middle
of the menstrual cycle, and of depression at the onset of menstruation. Mood swings in women are linked to a reduction in
the neurotransmitter serotonin, which drops and rises according
to estrogen levels. (As estrogen increases the demand for vitamin
B_6, intake of this vitamin will help the body maintain steady
levels of serotonin. Good sources are brewer's yeast, wheat germ,
and liver.)
(Mitchell, p. 39; Morgan, p. 20; Parade Magazine, 6/29/80, p. 24)

Motion Sickness
Females are more prone to motion sickness than males are. They
are most susceptible from two to twelve years of age, although
many adults are still afflicted. It is rare after the age of fifty.
(Fromer, p. 65)

Motivation for Playing Sports Among 10- to 18-year-old Youths

Boys are three times more likely than girls to state winning as their reason for competing in sports.

(*Monagan, p. 61 [from a survey by John Lewko]*)

Multiple Births

The tendency for multiple births is a trait carried by women, and is inherited. Nonidentical twins are the result of two ova (eggs) being fertilized by two sperm. Identical twins are the result of one ovum splitting after fertilization.

(*Woman's Body, pp. 92, 93*)

Multiple Sclerosis

Multiple sclerosis is a disease that seriously damages the sheaths that insulate the nerves. The average onset of multiple sclerosis is in the twenty-to-thirty-five-year-old range. More women than men suffer from it, in a ratio of three to two.

(*Hyman, p. 459*)

Mumps, Complications of

(Mumps is a viral disease in which there is painful swelling of the salivary glands.)

Male: In boys or men, there is a chance that the sex glands will also become inflamed, which can, in some cases, result in sterility.

Female: In the female, the ovaries may become inflamed producing pain and tenderness. However, there is no chance of sterility.

(*Smith, p. 231*)

Murder

One fourth of all murders are committed within the family.
One half of those are husband/wife killings.

(*Shearer, p. 18*)

Murder by Spouses

Male: In 1982 and 1983, 40 percent of the women murdered were killed by their spouses.

Female: Ten percent of the men murdered were killed by their spouses.

(*Time, 9/5/83, p. 23*)

Murder Victims
In 1979, of 19,260 murder victims, 77.1 percent (or 14,853) were male and 22.9 percent (or 4,407) were female.
(Hacker, p. 73)

Muscle Cells, Maximum Size of
Male: The muscle cells of a male increase in size until he is forty years old.
Female: The muscle cells of a woman reach their maximum size when she is about ten or eleven.
(Wagenvoord/Bailey, Women, p. 74)

Muscle Cells, Numbers of
Men have 50 percent more muscle cells than women. During puberty, the number of muscle cells in a woman increases ten times. During puberty, the number of muscle cells in a man increases twenty times.
(Wagenvoord/Bailey, Men, p. 84)

Muscle Fiber
Men have more muscle fiber than women, due to the activity of testosterone. Testosterone also adds bulk to muscles.
(Selden, p. 53)

Muscle Flexibility
Women have more muscle flexibility than men, due to the action of estrogen on the muscles.
(Cooley, p. 97)

Muscle Mass, Increase of
Due to hormonal differences, men can increase their muscle mass more rapidly than women can.
(Hammar, p. 10)

Muscle Percentage of Body Mass
Men: Forty percent of the male body is muscle.
Women: Thirty-five percent of a woman's body mass is muscle.
(Brothers, Woman's Day, 2/9/82, p. 138)

Muscles, Number of Voluntary
Both sexes have four hundred voluntary muscles.
(_Wagenvoord/Bailey_, Men, p. 70)

Muscles and Hormonal Differences
Hormonal differences are responsible for muscular variations in males and females.
(_Brothers_, Woman's Day, 2/9/82; p. 139)

Muscular Development
Male: Muscular development is stimulated by the male hormone testosterone, which increases greatly during adolescence.
Female: By contrast, female hormones inhibit the growth of muscles. Women can increase the strength of their muscles through vigorous exercise. A woman's arm muscles can develop up to 75 percent to 80 percent of the capacity of a man's, her lower legs can develop up to 70 percent of the strength of a man's, and the muscles of her hands and back can be about 60 percent as strong as a man's.
(_Dyer_, p. 109)

Muscular Dystrophy
(Muscular dystrophy is a disease characterized by muscle weakness and the eventual wasting away of the muscle tissue.) The most common form is called Duchenne. It affects boys, who usually die by the time they are twenty-five years old. The less common form occurs only in males but is inherited through female carriers. The carriers may experience some muscle weakness but do not actually have the disease.
(_Kunz_, pp. 694–5)

Muscular Strength in Adults
The muscular strength of women is about two-thirds that of men.
(_Billies_, p. 115)

Muscular Strength in Children
Most boys are stronger than most girls.
(Man's Body, pp. A16–18)

Museum Employees

Males: Eighty percent of the senior positions in museums are held by males.

Females: Twenty percent of the senior positions are held by women, though the majority of museum workers are women.

(Bird, p. 88)

Myasthenia Gravis

(This muscle disorder is one of the diseases in which the antibodies within one's body attack the body itself. Termed an autoimmune disease, symptoms include fatigue, loss of eye muscle control, and possibly the loss of control of the muscles that regulate breathing.)

Myasthenia gravis strikes young women and old men, and is seen more frequently in females.

(Science Digest, *September 1982, p. 90;* Health, *p. 22)*

Navy, Enlisted Personnel
6.5 percent of all enlisted navy personnel are female.
(Hacker, p. 207)

Navy, Officers
7.7 percent of all navy officers are female.
(Hacker, p. 207)

Nephritis
(A kidney disease.)
More men than women have nephritis.
(Brothers, Woman's Day, 2/9/82, p. 138)

Nerve Cells in the Brain
Both sexes have about ten billion nerve cells in the brain.
(Wagenvoord/Bailey, Men, p. 94)

Nervous System Differences in Babies
Males: The boy babies cry more often, are more fearful and more irritable than girls, eat more than girls, smile less than girls, and develop bowel and bladder control later than girls.
Females: Girl babies are more responsive to touch and light, have a keener sense of smell, are less fearful, less irritable, eat less, smile more often, develop bladder and bowel control earlier, and are more aware of their mother's presence earlier.
(Wagenvoord/Bailey, Men, p. 16)

Nervous System Diseases
More men than women contract diseases of the nervous system (such as muscular dystrophy and Lou Gehrig's disease).
(*Brothers*, Woman's Day, 2/9/82, p. 138)

Nervous System Infections
More men than women contract infections of the nervous system (such as encephalitis and syphilis).
(*Brothers*, Woman's Day, 2/9/82, p. 138)

Neurosurgeons
In general, women make better neurosurgeons due to their superiority at fine motor coordination.
(Newsweek, 5/18/81, p. 73)
Of the 396,000 neurosurgical operations performed in 1980, 50 percent were performed by females.
(*Hacker*, p. 82)

Newborns
Newborn males weigh an average of five ounces more, have stronger grips and more muscular forearms, and are an average of one half inch longer than newborn females.
(*Wagenvoord/Bailey*, Men, p. 81)

News, Sexes Featured on
Males: In 1977, 90 percent of the news featured males.
Females: Ten percent of the news featured females.
(*Bird*, p. 143)

Newspaper Editors and Reporters
57.6 percent of newspaper editors and reporters are male.
(*Department of Labor*, 1979)

Nondrinkers
More women than men are nondrinkers.
Males: Twenty-one percent of men are nondrinkers.
Females: 34.2 percent of women are nondrinkers.
(Geosphere, *August 1981*, p. 142)

Nonspecific Urethritis

Male: This is the most common sexual disorder in men. Symptoms include discharge and discomfort when urinating. If untreated, it can spread to other organs and sometimes causes permanent damage to eyes or joints.

Female: Symptoms in women are barely noticeable. Complications are rare in females.

(Woman's Body, *p. 377*)

Nonverbal Cues as to the Feelings of Others

Women are considered better than men at recognizing what another person is feeling.

(*Brothers*, Woman's Day, *2/9/82, p. 142*)

Nuclear Power, Support for

More men than women are in favor of nuclear power. Some authorities feel this is due to women's feelings that nuclear plants are a threat to health and safety.

(*Cory, "Newsline,"* Psychology Today, *November 1981, p. 25; Researcher, Charles Brody*)

Nursery School and Kindergarten Teachers

98.4 percent of nursery school and kindergarten teachers are female.

(*Hacker, p. 127*)

Nursery School Teachers and Behavior

Male nursery school teachers are more affectionate than female teachers, and are more likely to communicate support to children.

(*Researcher: Beverly Fagot,* Psychology Today, *November 1981, p. 25*)

Nurses, Practical

97.5 percent of practical nurses are female.

(*Hacker, p. 127*)

Nurses, Registered

96.7 percent of registered nurses are female.

(*Department of Labor, 1979*)

Nursing, Doctorates
Male: In 1980, two doctorate degrees in nursing were awarded to men.
Female: One hundred thirteen doctorates in nursing were awarded to women in 1980.
(U.S. Statistics, p. 166)

Nursing, Master's Degrees
Male: 158 master's degrees in nursing were awarded to men in 1980.
Female: 4,548 master's degrees in nursing were awarded to women.
(U.S. Statistics, p. 166)

Nursing Homes
Male: In 1979, 378,000 men resided in nursing homes.
Female: In the same year, 803,000 women resided in nursing homes.
(Census, 1981, p. 114)

Nurturers
Women are perceived as being more nurturing than men.
(Adams, p. 75)

Obesity
Males: When more than 25 percent of a man's body is composed of fat, he is termed obese.
Females: A woman whose body is composed of more than 30 percent fat is labeled obese.
  (*Wilmore, p. 75*)

Obesity and Age
Males: Fourteen percent of all men from ages twenty to forty-four are obese.
Females: Twenty percent of all females from ages twenty to forty-four are obese. Thirty percent of all females from ages forty-five to seventy-five are obese.
  (*Kaufman, p. 77*)

Obesity and Diabetes
Males: The more a man weighs, the greater his risk of contracting diabetes.
Females: Those women who gain weight in the neck, shoulders, and abdomen have a high risk of developing diabetes.
  (*Kissebah, p. 54*)

Obesity and Location of Fat Storage
Males: Males usually store excess calories as fat in the stomach, neck, and shoulders.
Females: Females usually store fat in the thighs, hips, buttocks, and stomach.
  (*Kissebah, p. 54*)

Obstructive Sleep Apnea
(This is a potentially life-threatening breathing disorder characterized by an involuntary cutoff of air occurring during sleep.)
   Although obstructive sleep apnea affects both men and women, it is most common in older obese men.
   (Prevention, 1/83, p. 38)

Odor, Body
Body odor on a man is usually stronger than that on a woman. Two possible reasons for this are that a man does not shave under his arms and hair tends to harbor bacteria, which results in odor; and men sweat more than women.
   (Wagenvoord/Bailey, Men, p. 75)

Odors
Women are more sensitive to odors than men are.
   (Wagenvoord/Bailey, Men, p. 96)

Office-Machine Repairers
93.7 percent of office-machine repairers are male.
   (Hacker, p. 128)

Older and Feeling Better
Both males and females age fifty-five and over report feeling much better than younger people.
   (Rubinstein, Psychology Today, Health Survey, October 1982, p. 32)

Older People, Psychological Characteristics of the Retired
Older women report more depression, loneliness, and anxiety than older men.
   (Atchley and Seltzer, p. 286)

Older People and Marriage
Thirty-five thousand older men and sixteen thousand older women wed each year.
   (Kart and Manard, p. 203)

Older People and Sex
The Kinsey Report indicates that four out of five men over the age of sixty are quite capable of having sexual relations, and that

there is no sign of sexual decline in women. The Starr-Weiner study reports that a woman of eighty has the same orgasmic potential as a woman of twenty.

   (Starr-Weiner, p. 80; Kart and Manard, p. 205)

Oldest People

Males: In 1983 the oldest man living was Shigechiyo Izumi of Japan, who was 116 years old.

   (Georgakas, p. 37)

Females: The oldest known woman whose age has been recorded and verified was Delina Filkins of New York, who lived to be 113 years and 214 days old.

   (Georgakas, p. 25)

Olympic Competition

Women are not allowed to participate in nine of the twenty-seven Olympic Sports categories: boxing, soccer, judo, wrestling, the pentathlon, weight lifting, the biathlon, bobsledding, and ice hockey. Fifteen events are male/female competitive. One hundred sixty-eight events are restricted to males, seventy-eight are restricted to females.

   (Ross, p. 19)

Olympic Committee, International

Male: Eighty-six men sit on the IOC.

Female: Three women sit on this committee. (Until 1981, no women were included.)

   (Ross, p. 19)

Operations

Five million more women than men have operations.

   (Murphy, p. 50)

Optometry Degrees

Male: In the 1979–80 academic year, 84.3 percent of optometry degrees were awarded to men.

Female: 15.7 percent were awarded to women.

   (Hacker, p. 244)

Orgasm, Arousal Time for
Males: Men are aroused more quickly than women, and can reach orgasm in a matter of seconds.
Females: Women are generally believed to respond more slowly than men (taking from ten to twenty minutes) to both arousal and climax. (This does not apply to masturbation, so many people feel—and some research shows—that a woman's slower response time to arousal is learned.)
(*Tavris and Sadd, p. 208*)

Orgasm, Description of
Both sexes describe the experience of orgasm in similar terms. However, while the experiences of men are similar each time, women may have a variety of types of orgasms ranging from weak to very intense.
(*Tavris and Sadd, pp. 202, 203*)

Orgasm, During Sleep
Both sexes report this occurrence. Among women the experience occurs more frequently with age.
(Woman's Body, *p. 42*)

Orgasm, Heights of, and Age
Males: Men are believed to reach the heights, both of their desire for sex and the intensity of the orgasm, in their late teens.
Females: Females are believed to reach the heights of both sexual need and pleasure in their mid-thirties.
(*Gross, p. 207*)

Orgasm, Inability to Achieve
Men: There is no specific information as to the numbers of men who are unable to achieve orgasm, either in terms of inability to achieve erection or to achieve orgasm with an erection. Authorities believe that most men experience this inability temporarily at one time or another during their lives.
Women: There are numerous reports on the numbers of women who never reach orgasm. *The Hite Report,* for instance, indicates that 12 percent never do. *Redbook* cites an incidence of 7 percent, *Cosmopolitan* 10 percent, and Starr-Weiner 1.5 percent.
(Woman's Body, *p. 34; Starr-Weiner, p. 50*)

Orgasms, Multiple
Both sexes report multiple orgasms, although it is more common among women.
Male: Each male orgasm is a distinct entity. The ability to achieve multiple orgasms is at its peak in adolescent boys and declines with age in the male.
Female: Multiple orgasms in females are all a part of one orgasm, experienced as waves, with each one blending into the last. Kinsey reported that 14 percent of women with experience could have three to five orgasms within a few minutes.
(*Wagenvoord/Bailey, Men, p. 133*)

Orgasms, Number of Prior to Marriage
Males: Men were found to have an average of 1,523 orgasms prior to marriage.
Females: Women were found to have had some 223 orgasms prior to marriage. (This is "old research" from the Kinsey Report [1953]. There were no similar data available through 1982, but many authorities think those numbers are now much larger!)
(*Kinsey Report*)

Osteoarthritis
This is a degenerative joint disease causing pain and swelling in the joints. It occurs in 80 percent to 90 percent of the people over the age of sixty, and in men more than in women.
(*Woman's Body, p. 407*)

Osteoporosis
Osteoporosis brings about a gradual thinning of the bones. It is usually painless until a sudden fall results in a fracture. One of four women will suffer a fracture of the wrist or hip as a result of the disease. Women have four times the rate of the disease as men do, and one in six women will die as a result of related injuries.
(*Pascoe, p. 90*)

Osteosclerosis
(Osteosclerosis is the progressive development of deafness, first in one ear and then in the other. It is caused by an overgrowth of tissue in the middle ear, resulting in the freezing of the bones in the middle ear.)

Osteosclerosis occurs most often in women before the age of thirty, and afflicts one in two hundred fifty people.

(Woman's Body, p. 235)

Ova and Sperms, Numbers of

Males: The testes do not begin producing sperm until puberty and they then produce them at a rate of 10 to 30 billion per month, or 1,000 million per week.

Females: A female's ovaries contain about 350,000 immature eggs or ova at birth. Only about four hundred of them ever mature.

(Hyman, pp. 311, 317)

Overweight, Average

Males: The average American male is twenty to thirty pounds overweight.

Females: The average American female is fifteen to thirty pounds overweight. There are more overweight women than overweight men.

(Kaufman, p. 77)

Overweight and Job Discrimination

It is more important for a woman than for a man to be slim when looking for a job.

(Sandler, p. 29)

Oxygen Efficiency

Men have larger hearts and lungs, which are able to pump blood and oxygen to the muscles more efficiently than women's hearts and lungs can.

(Billies, p. 115)

Oxygen Needs

Men need more oxygen than women do, as they breathe more deeply.

(Brothers, p. 22)

Oxygen Pulse

(Oxygen pulse is a measurement used to determine how effectively one's heart functions as a respiratory organ, taking into consideration such factors as blood volume, hemoglobin content, and body weight.)

(Klafs and Arnheim, p. 183)

At age fifteen, oxygen pulse is equal in the sexes, but men go on to double their oxygen pulse by the early twenties while that of women stays the same.

(Hammar, p. 9)

Oxygen Uptake

(Oxygen uptake is defined as the efficiency with which the body takes in oxygen.)

Men can attain between 15 percent and 24 percent more oxygen uptake than women during physical exertion.

(Dyer, p. 110)

P

Pain
Women feel more pain than men do (i.e., they are more sensitive to pain than men).
(*Buchsbaum, p. 98*)

Painters
There are more male painters than female.
(*Goleman, p. 59*)

Parkinson's Disease
This affliction, which is characterized by trembling and muscular rigidity due to the degeneration of nerve cells in one part of the brain, occurs more often in men than in women.
(*Woman's Body, p. 405*)

Part-time Year-round Employees
22.1 percent of all wage and salary earners worked on a part-time basis in 1977.
(*Nollen, p. 5*)
Males: 55.8 percent of those working part time in 1981 were male.
Females: 44.2 percent of those who worked part time in 1981 were female.
(*Hacker, p. 118*)

Pattern Baldness
Males: This kind of balding becomes most apparent after age

forty. Beginning in the late twenties, hair recedes gradually, culminating in hair loss on the entire head except for a fringe of hair that persists around the sides and back of the head. Authorities feel that the baldness is caused by a combination of hormones, age, and heredity.

Females: The common thinning that occurs in older women is called androgenic hair loss, or masculine hair loss, resembling male pattern baldness.

(*Cooley, p. 41*)

Pedestrians, Deaths
More men than women have died in pedestrian accidents.

(Psychology Today, *January 1983, p. 4*)

Pedophilia (Sex with Children)
Child molesters are men in 97 percent of the reported cases. Two hundred to three hundred men for every one woman are prosecuted for child molesting.

(*Sanford, p. 83*)

Pelvis
Males: The male pelvis is heavier and thicker than the woman's.
Females: The woman's pelvis is, on the average, two inches wider than a man's.

(*Selden, p. 53*)

Penis Envy and Vagina Envy
Males: According to certain psychoanalytic theories, men envy women's ability to give birth.
Females: Women are envious of the power and domination represented by the penis.

(*Brenner, p. 122*)

Perception, Three-dimensional
Boys do better than girls on tests that involve three-dimensional perception.

(*Wagenvoord/Bailey,* Women, *p. 24*)

Perception of Subliminal Messages
In various studies, females have been found to be better than males at perceiving subliminal messages.

(*Brothers*, Woman's Day, 2/9/82, p. 142)

Perceptiveness
Females are considered more perceptive than men. According to numerous studies, females are better able to sense the thoughts and future actions of others than men are. More recent studies attribute this to the theory that women utilize both sides of their brains, whereas men are more specialized and utilize only one side at a time for specific matters.

(*Eppingham*, p. 37)

Permissive Women
Both men and women rate permissive females as being more irresponsible, immature, immoral, and insecure than other kinds of females.

(*Researchers: Louis Janda, Old Dominion University, Norfolk, Virginia; Kevin O'Grady and Sherry Namhart, assisting*)

Personality Traits and Intellectual Achievement
Males: Boys who are intellectually outstanding are often timid, anxious, not overly aggressive, and less active than other boys. *Females:* Girls whose intellectual achievements are the greatest tend to be unusually active, independent, competitive, and free of anxiety or fear.

(*Researchers: Eleanor Maccaby and Carol Nagly Jachlin, Stanford University*)

Perspiration
Males tend to perspire more than females. However, after menopause, women do perspire more than previously.

(*Selden*, p. 53)

Persuadability
Women and men are equally persuadable.

(*"Let's Put Our Heads Together,"* p. 22)

Pharmacy Students
Slightly less than half of pharmacy students are female.

(*Boyd*, p. E18, 12/15/83)

Ph.D.s (Doctorates)
Males earned 70 percent of the doctorates awarded in 1983.
    (Murphy, p. 50)

Pheromones
Pheromones are body odors containing certain chemicals that, among lower animals such as dogs and cats, stimulate the opposite sex sexually. It is not clear if this sensitivity exists in humans. Some studies indicate that it does, and that males secrete a substance that can be detected by fertile females.
    (Wagenvoord/Bailey, Women, pp. 78–79)

Phobias
(A phobia is a special form of fear that cannot be controlled voluntarily, cannot be explained away, and leads to avoidance of the feared situation, such as agoraphobia [fear of open spaces] and claustrophobia [fear of confined spaces].)
    Twice as many women as men are phobic.
    (Franks and Burtle, pp. 132–168)

Phobias, Animal
More women than men have animal phobias.
    (Franks and Burtle, p. 136)

Physical Attractiveness and High Blood Pressure Reading in College and High School
Male: No blood pressure differences were noted between attractive and unattractive men in college or high school.
Female: Attractive females in college and high school had lower blood pressure readings than unattractive girls.
    (Researcher: Stephan Hansell, Johns Hopkins University)

Physical Attractiveness as an Attribute Sought for in a Mate
More men than women consider physical attractiveness a prerequuisite for a mate.
    (Wilder, p. 5)

Physical Capacities During the Fifties
Males: A man in his late fifties can do only 60 percent of the physical work he could do in his forties. The strength of his back muscles declines over 90 percent after age fifty; the amount of

oxygen he can carry in his blood declines; and the air sacs in his lungs thicken.

(*Wagenvoord/Bailey*, Men, p. 154)

Females: A female in her late fifties can, if trained, maintain about 90 percent of the exercise capacity she had when she was twenty. Women also often experience a "postmenopausal zest," experienced as renewed energy and interest in the world. There is a 2 percent per year bone loss in women, beginning after about age thirty-five or earlier, which should be monitored and aided through exercise and adequate calcium intake.

(*Brothers*, Woman's Day, 2/9/82, p. 58; *Cooley*, p. 459)

Physical Capacities During the Forties

Males: A man in his forties is at the peak of his endurance capacity. The oxygen-carrying capacity of his blood is at its peak and his muscles are strong. He is also usually at the peak of his career.

(*Wagenvoord/Bailey*, Men, p. 153)

Females: The female in her forties is beginning to notice gray hairs and a few wrinkles. Blood pressure may increase due to the decreasing of the elasticity cf the aorta and major blood vessels. Estrogen may be waning and women may notice some changes in digestion, a redistribution of fat, and a change of the body shape. The capacity to exercise remains close to that of a twenty-year-old woman. Women may begin to notice the signs of menopause, such as fatigue, sleeplessness, irregular periods, appetite variations, hot flashes; or they may feel no discomfort at all.

(Ms., Man's Body, Woman's Body)

Physical Closeness

Males: Men tend to behave aggressively when seated close to one another.

Females: Women often experience greater intimacy when seated close to one another.

(Human Behavior, March 1978, p. 27)

Physical Sciences, Doctorates

Male: In the 1979–80 academic year, 87.7 percent of doctorates in the physical sciences went to men.

Female: 12.3 percent were awarded to women.

(*Hacker*, p. 244)

Physical Therapists
In 1984 about 70 percent of physical therapists were female.
(D. Rubin, p. 63)

Physicians
Males: In 1984, 85.2 percent of physicians were male.
Females: 14.8 percent of physicians were female.
(D. Rubin, p. 63)

Physicians, Male, and Attitude Toward Sex of Patients
Male physicians take medical illness more seriously in men than in women, and give men more extensive medical exams.
(Journal of American Medical Association, *and Frankfort, pp. 24–25*)

Physicians, Teaching
Female physicians are more likely than male physicians to teach.
(Kirk and Rosenblatt, p. 435)

Physicians, Visits to
In 1979, 58.7 percent of those who visited physicians were female, and 41.3 percent were male. Women averaged 5.4 visits per year, and men averaged 4.1.
(Hacker, p. 79)

Physicians and Administrators as Health Policy Makers
Male: Ninety percent of those making health policy are male.
Female: Ten percent of those making health policy decisions are female.
(Bird, p. 128)

Physicians and Sex of Patient
Male: 60.1 percent of the patients visiting male physicians are female.
Female: Women patients account for 71.5 percent of the visits to female physicians.
(Hacker, p. 86)

Physicians and Time Spent with Patients
Male physicians spend an average of 15.3 minutes with each patient, in contrast to female physicians, who spend an average of 17.8 minutes with each patient.
(Hacker, p. 198)

Physicians Who Have Sexual Contact with Patients
Very few male physicians have sexual contact with patients, and almost no female physicians do.

(*"Crosstalk,"* Psychology Today, *February 1983, p. 14*)

Physiology of Sexuality
Both sexes progress through four distinct stages of physical responsiveness to sexual arousal: excitement, plateau, orgasm, and resolution (see *Sexual Response*).

(Woman's Body, *p. 29*)

Picture Completion
Tests indicate that men are better than females at picture completion. Twenty-five percent of the women do as well as 75 percent of the men at these kinds of tasks.

(*Researcher: Phillip Braydon, Ph.D., University of Waterloo, Ontario*)

Pill
Male: There is now a birth-control pill for men being utilized in China. It is made from gossypol and is said to be relatively safe. This antifertility pill does not impair potency, and fertility can be restored within three months after use is discontinued. Apparently it does not cause cancer.

Female: Two kinds of birth-control pills are available. Both work by preventing ovulation (release of an ovum), so that pregnancy cannot occur.

(*Cooke and Dworkin, p. 40;* New Woman, *September–October 1980, p. 14*)

Pilots
Male: In 1982, 796,000 of the licensed airplane pilots in the U.S.A. were male.

Female: 8,000 were women.

(*Kantel, p. 11*)

Pink-Collar Profession
When a particular profession is made up of 80 percent or more women, with a low percentage of men (such as nursing), it is called a "pink-collar" profession. Members of pink-collar professions are generally poorly paid. Eighty percent of women work in pink-collar professions.

(Time, *7/12/82*)

Pistols, Possession of
In 1981, 33 percent of the men polled (compared to 45 percent of the women) favored a legal ban on pistols and revolvers except for possession by police and other authorities related to the law.
   (Tobias and Leader, p. 122)

Plastic Surgery
Twenty percent to 30 percent of the patients seeking plastic surgery in larger cities are men.
   (Brothers, p. 65)

Play
Boys play more roughly than girls. Some feel this is because males of all species are more aggressive. Others feel it is because boys are expected to play rough. (It is probably a combination of both.)
   ("Ideas," Newsweek, 5/18/81, p. 72)

Pleasure
Both men and women get more pleasure from reading than from fourteen other activities, including playing golf, working outside the home, and attending a party. After reading, the activities men enjoy most are golf and sports events, while women enjoy driving, cooking, smoking cigarettes, and flying.
   (U.S.A. Today, 6/7/83, p. 1)

Plumbers
In 1981, 99.4 percent of plumbers were male.
   (Hacker, p. 127)

Pneumonia
More men than women suffer from pneumonia.
   (Brothers, Woman's Day, 2/9/82, p. 138)

Poets and Writers, Directory of
Male: Seventy-nine percent of the listings in the *Directory of Poets and Writers* (1977) are male.
Female: Twenty-one percent are women.
   (Bird, p. 87)

Police Officers
In 1981, 94.5 percent of the police officers were male.
(Hacker, p. 128)

Polio
Males are more susceptible to polio than females are.
("Mind and Body," Science Digest, September 1982, p. 90)

Political Campaign Photographs
In photographs used in political campaigns, potential voters prefer to see a woman's face and body but just a man's face.
(Cory, Psychology Today, January 1981, p. 31)

Political Dominance
The male sex is politically dominant all over the world.
(Nardi, p. 1158)

Political Preference
Women tend to be more liberal and democratically oriented than men.
(Murphy, p. 50)

Polygamy (Having more than one spouse)
In a study of 853 human societies, the practice of having only one wife was the norm in only 16 percent of them. Among the remaining eighty-four percent, polygamy is considered acceptable. Polyandry (when a woman takes more than one husband) occurred in 0.5 percent of them.
(Science Digest, July 1982, p. 64)

Polymyalgia Rheumatica
(This disease is rare in people under age fifty. Its symptoms include pain and stiffness upon rising that lasts well into the day. The pain seems to begin in the neck, shoulders, and hips. Fatigue and weight and appetite loss are accompanying symptoms. Treatment with the drug prednisone is effective.)

Polymyalgia rheumatica affects twice as many women as men.
(Bennett, p. 2)

Population
Male: In 1981, 110 million people in the U.S.A. were male.
Female: 116.5 million people in the U.S.A. were female.
(U.S.A. Statistics in Brief, *1981, p. 145*)

Pornography and Homosexuals
There is no significant pornography market for lesbians, but male homosexuals purchase substantial amounts of pornographic material.
(*Symonds, p. 86*)

Possessions, Cherished, of the Aged
Male: Radios, books, and television sets are the most cherished items of older men.
Female: Photographs are the most cherished possessions of older women.
(*"Aging,"* Human Behavior, *July 1978, p. 37*)

Postmenopausal Zest (Term coined by Margaret Mead)
Males: Older men do not seem to experience the zest reported by women after menopause. After fifty, men are reportedly "more tired."
Females: Women seem to have a great deal of energy after menopause. This may be a combination of biological factors and the woman's social situation. Usually by this time, children have left home and she is free to achieve something outside the family.
(*Mitchell, p. 166*)

Poverty, Families
Males: In 1978, 5.9 percent of all poor families were headed by single males.
Females: 35.6 percent of all poor families were headed by single females. (50.6 percent of all black, female-headed families, were poor.) The remaining poor families were headed by a couple.
(*U.S. Bureau of the Census, 1978;* Almanac, *p. 13*)
One half of all families below the poverty line in 1980 were maintained by women.
(Time, *7/12/83, p. 24*)

Power, and Sexual Stability in Relationships

Males: Men with a greater desire for power than most are more discontent with their love lives and show less affection for their partners. The researchers of this study concluded that men who have a great need for power have difficulty establishing stable relationships with women.

Females: Women with a greater need for power do not have less stable romantic relationships than those who show much less desire for power.

    (Researchers: Abigail Stewart, Ph.D., Boston University, and Zick Rubin, M.D., Ph.D., Harvard University; Human Behavior, April 1977, p. 37)

Power, in Love Relationships, What the Sexes Say They Want

Male: Eighty-seven percent of the men surveyed said they favored a relationship in which both male and female had equal power.

Female: Ninety-five percent of the women said they favored equality in a relationship with a member of the opposite sex.

    (Peplau, Rubin, and Hill, p. 142)

Power, in Relationships, What People Do

Male: Forty-two percent of the men polled thought they had equal power in a relationship. Three quarters of those remaining felt they were the dominant partner.

Female: Forty-nine percent of the women polled said they were equal in terms of power to the man in their relationship. Two thirds of those remaining felt the man "had the final say."

    (Peplau, Rubin, and Hill, p. 147)

Power, in the Office

Women with the same education and the same occupation status as men are less likely than men to be in powerful positions in the office.

    (Researchers: Wendy Wolf, Ph.D. and Neil D. Fligstein, Ph.D., University of Wisconsin)

Power, Need for

There is no difference between the sexes in terms of what many feel is a basic human need for power.

    (Researchers: Stewart and Zubin, Human Behavior, April 1977, p. 37)

Pregnancy
A woman who is pregnant with a male may experience a shorter pregnancy than if tho baby is a female.
(Man's Body, pp. A05–06)

Premarital Violence Among College Students
Three studies, undertaken in Oregon, Minnesota, and Arizona, revealed that physical abuse occurs in one out of every five dating relationships. Most victims of the abuse are women.
(In Response to Violence in the Family, July/August, 1981, Vol. 4, No. 6, p. 1)

Premature Infants
(Premature is defined as an infant who weighs less than five pounds at birth.)
Because girls are usually lighter in weight, there are more premature females than males.
(Woman's Body, p. 7)

Prenatal Problems
Male babies are more likely to suffer from prenatal problems than female babies.
(Brothers, Woman's Day, 2/9/82, p. 60)

Presidential Appointees (Senate-approved)
Male: Six hundred twenty-seven of President Reagan's appointees are men.
Female: Fifty-five are women.
(Field, p. 78, 1982)

Prison Populations, Federal and State
The total prison population in 1981 was 349,118.
Male: 95.8 percent, or 334,462, were men.
Female: 4.2 percent, or 14,656, were women.
(Hacker, p. 228)

Prisons, State
Male: There are two hundred fifty state prisons for men.
Female: There are forty state prisons for women.
(Bird, p. 153)

Prison Services
Women and girls in institutions have less recreation, less counseling, less vocational training, and spend longer periods of time
institutionalized than do men or boys.
  (*Bird, p. 153*)

Privates in the Armed Forces
In 1981, of 673,448 privates in the armed forces, 77,872 were
female.
  (*Hacker, p. 206*)

Problem Solving
Males: Men are better problem solvers when the problems are
quite specific.
Females: Women are more "globally minded" and do better at
solving general problems.
  (*Newseek, 5/18/81, p. 81*)
Scientists feel this is due to the differences in brain structure.
Men's brains are more specialized than women's brains, and in-
formation is filtered into one side or the other. In a woman's
brain information and other stimuli are received by both sides at
once.
  (*Goleman, p. 34*)

Processing Information
Women process information faster than men because of their
brain structures.
  (*Goleman, p. 59*)

Professors
In 1984, 35.4 percent of university and college professors were
female.
  (*D. Rubin, p. 62*)

Progesterone
Progesterone is a hormone found in both males and females, but
in differing amounts at various times. It is found in very low
amounts in the female until ovulation (the release of the egg),
after which her levels may exceed the male's by as much as five
to one hundred times, depending on age, individual differences,

and the stage of the menstrual cycle. Progesterone, produced in women by the ovaries, is responsible for breast development and for the maintenance of the uterine lining during pregnancy. It is this hormone that is responsible for suppressing ovulation during pregnancy, which is why it is used in birth-control pills.

(*Behrman and Vaughn, p. 1846; Mitchell, p. 11; Money, p. 201; Wagenvoord/ Bailey,* Women, *p. 156*)

Prolactin

Prolactin is a hormone produced by both sexes. It is found in the tears of the emotionally upset and its production increases during times of stress.

Males: Men produce substantial amounts of prolactin. Significantly smaller amounts are found in impotent men and men suffering from premature ejaculation.

Females: Prolactin is essential for human milk production and lactation.

(*Cooke and Dworkin, p. 171; Kotulak, p. A13; Mitchell, p. 66*)

Promiscuity

Some say that both promiscuous males and females are actually seeking a loving parent.

(*Scarf, p. 87*)

Women are less promiscuous than men.

(*Collier, p. 86*)

Promotions (Job) in Financial Industry

Women are promoted more often than men in the financial industry, but the promotions are relatively small and insignificant so that females tend to remain in lower positions. Men are promoted less frequently, but rise higher on the success ladder.

(*"Crosstalk,"* Psychology Today, *February 1983, p. 14*)

Prostaglandins

Prostaglandins are potent chemicals produced by many tissues in the body.

Male: Prostaglandins are found in the prostate gland (hence their name) in men, and are present in seminal fluid.

Female: Prostaglandins trigger uterine contractions at menses, labor, and delivery, and are present in menstrual discharge.

(*Money, p. 22; Kirschmann, p. 57*)

Protein Needs

Males: Men between the ages of eleven and fifty-one need from forty-five to fifty-six grams of protein daily.

Females: Women between the ages of eleven and fifty-one need about forty-one to forty-five grams of protein daily.

    (Luna, p. 60)

Psychiatric Patients, Outpatient

More female than male psychiatric patients are treated on an out-patient basis.

    (DeRosis and Pelligrino, p. 3)

Psychiatrists

Males: In 1982, 80 percent of all psychiatrists were male.

Females: Twenty percent were female.

    (Kirk and Rosenblatt, p. 431)

Psychological Anxiety

Many studies (including Bernard's *The Future of Marriage*) and studies from the University of Michigan's Institute for Social Research, as well as the *Psychology Today* (October 1982) survey, indicate that women experience more psychological anxiety than men. The reasons given for this are both cultural (that women have not been afforded the same opportunities as men), and realistic (that today's woman is expected to be able to manage a job as well as to care for the children and her husband). Even though the "Superwoman" image is supposedly dead, the reality is that most women must handle at least two jobs if they are married or have children. The other side of the coin is that some studies indicate that married women, although filled with anxiety, are still healthier physically than unmarried women. Working women are also healthier than nonworking women. The answer to the dilemma may be that the working mother has both a family to love and by whom she is loved and needed, and the chance to fulfill her potential goals as an individual. Although society has not found the balance as yet, the "new male" (a male who shares the responsibilities of the children and household) who is making his appearance may provide it. So the future may be a very bright one for both men and women.

    (Jane Stump)

Psychology, Doctorates in
Male: In 1980, 1,618 doctorates in psychology were awarded to men.
Female: 1,155 doctorates in psychology were awarded to women in 1980.
(U.S. Statistical Abstract, *p. 166*)

Psychology, Master's Degrees in
Male: In 1980, 3,409 master's degrees in psychology were awarded to men.
Female: In 1980, 4,486 master's degrees in psychology were awarded to women.
(U.S. Statistical Abstract, *p. 166*)

Psychosomatic Illness
More women than men are diagnosed as suffering from psychosomatic illnesses.
(Horn, *December 1977*, Psychology Today, *p. 152*)

Puberty
(Puberty is the time during which the process of sexual maturation takes place.)
Males: When sperm are produced in the male, puberty has begun. Boys usually enter puberty from ages ten to fourteen, and complete development between ages fourteen and eighteen. At puberty boys experience an upward shift in blood pressure and increased levels of triglycerides (a blood fat), and lower levels of high-density lipoproteins (elements that whisk fat out of the body so it doesn't accumulate on artery walls.)
Females: When a woman begins to produce ova and menses commence, puberty has begun. In girls, this usually occurs at ages nine to fourteen and is completed from ages fourteen to eighteen. At this time a girl's insulin levels rise, as one of the tasks of insulin is to "lay down fat."
(Woman's Body, *pp. 12, 13; Foley, p. 59*)

Pubic Hair
Pubic hair on the woman grows in a horizontal line, in contrast to the male growth, which grows up toward the navel.
(*Wagenvoord/Bailey*, Men, *p. 84*)

Androgens, or male hormones found in both males and females, are responsible for both underarm and pubic hair.

(*Mitchell, p. 29*)

Public Relations Workers
Males and females are equally represented in public relations jobs.

(*D. Rubin, p. 63*)

Pulse Rate
After age ten, females have consistently higher pulse rates than males.

(*Hammar, p. 9*)

Women have a greater and more rapid increase in pulse rate at the beginning of exercise and a slower recovery rate than men.

(*Klafs and Arnheim, p. 183*)

Pulse Rates of Athletes
The pulse rate of the female athlete is about ten beats slower per minute than that of a male athlete.

(*Klafs and Arnheim, p. 183*)

Push-ups
Males: Men should be able to do eight to ten push-ups.
Females: Women should be able to do four to six push-ups.

(YMCA Physical Fitness Standards Handbook, *cited by Lance, p. 38*)

Quadruplets

Quadruplets may be the result of a woman's releasing four or more eggs instead of just one, or of two ova splitting more than once. Multiple births tend to be an inherited trait, carried by women rather than men.

(Woman's Body, *p. 92*)

R

Rape Fantasies
According to numerous studies, both sexes have fantasies of being raped by the opposite sex.
(Human Behavior, *November 1978, p. 50)*

Ratios, Male to Female, Worldwide
Throughout the world, there are one hundred men for every one hundred women. In Asia, Africa, and the Middle East, men outnumber women. In the United States and Western Europe, women outnumber men, except in Alaska, where men outnumber women.
(Man's Body, *pp. A31–32)*

Reaction Time
Men have faster reaction times than women.
(Newsweek, *5/18/81, p. 73)*

Reading
Girls master reading earlier than boys do.
(Goleman, *p. 59)*

Real Estate Brokers and Agents
Fifty-five percent of real estate brokers and agents are male.
(Department of Labor, *1979)*

Rearing a Child, Cost of
It costs about $75,000 to rear a child of either sex.
(Brothers, *p. 39)*

Receptionists
96.3 percent of receptionists are female.
  (Hacker, p. 127)

Red Blood Cells, Average Number of
Male: A man has an average of 5 million red blood cells per cubic millimeter of blood.
Female: A woman has about 4.5 million red blood cells per cubic millimeter.
  (Klafs and Arnheim, p. 183)

Relationship with the Opposite Sex, Fear of
Male: Men fear they will either be smothered by a close relationship with a woman or they will be rejected.
Female: Women fear competition or that they will be left alone.
  (Gilligan, p. 71)

Relaxin
The sex hormone relaxin softens and stretches the ligaments that attach muscles to bones. Women produce more of this hormone than men do. This is why a woman's body is so much more flexible than a man's.
  (Dyer, p. 109)

Religion
More women than men say they believe in God. Women also attend church more regularly.
  (Eppingham, p. 37)

Remarriage after Divorce
Seventy-three percent of divorced people remarry.
Male: 78.3 percent of divorced men remarry.
Female: 68.8 percent of divorced women remarry. Of women who get divorced prior to age thirty, 76.3 percent remarry. Of those who get divorced at fifty or older, only 11.5 percent remarry. (No comparable figures are available for men.)
  (Hacker, pp. 112, 113)

Remarriage of Divorced Women, Median Age for
Male: The median age of divorced men who marry divorced women is 35.3 years.
Female: The median age of divorced women who remarry is 31.9 years.
   (*Hacker, p. 104*)

Remarriage of the Widowed, Median Age for
Male: The median age at which widowers remarry is 61.9 years.
Female: The median age at which widows remarry is 55.2 years.
   (*Hacker, p. 104*)

Remedial Reading Classes
Males outnumber females in remedial reading classes.
   (*Goleman, p. 120*)

Reproduction and Orgasm
The male must have an orgasm for reproduction to occur. It is not necessary for the female to experience orgasm in order to conceive.
   (*Man's Body, p. 131*)

Reproductive Capacity and Age
Males: There is no age limit for the male in terms of reproduction.
Females: After the menopause the female is infertile and incapable of pregnancy.
   (*Hyman, p. 436*)

Reproductive Cycles, Peak Season
Both male and female reproductive cycles seem to function at their peaks in the fall.
   (*Glassman, p. 76*)

Research in Medicine
Women physicians are just as likely as men to be researchers.
   (*Kirk and Rosenblatt, p. 432*)

Respiratory Illness, Influenza and Pneumonia
Men experience respiratory illness, influenza, and pneumonia more often than women do.
(Science Digest, *September 1982, p. 90*)

Retarded Persons, Institutions for
There are more men than women in institutions for the retarded.
(Parlee, p. 66)

Retirement
There are more retired women than retired men.
(Woman's Body, *p. 411*)

Retirement, Adaptation to
Most men and women like retirement and become adapted to it in a very short time. Older men are more likely than older women to become accustomed to retirement in three months or less.
(Atchley and Seltzer, pp. 287, 288)

Retirement and Identity Crisis
Male: Many men face an identity crisis when they retire, as their self-image and esteem is most often derived from working.
Female: Women usually do not experience the crisis men do at retirement, as their self-worth is associated with caring for the home as well as with their paying jobs.
(Woman's Body, *p. 411*)

Rheumatism
Women are two times as likely as men to develop rheumatism.
(Man's Body, *pp. C05–06*)

Rheumatoid Arthritis
This disorder of the joints affects more women than men. Beginning in middle age, it becomes more severe with age as the tissues in the joints become very thick and destroy the cartilage. The joint then becomes swollen and may become fused.
(Woman's Body, *p. 407*)

Rich, Feeling
Male: For a male to feel rich, he would need to have from half a million to a million dollars.
Female: For a woman to feel rich, she would need from $50,000 to $100,000.
(*Rubinstein, p. 39*)

Richer and Fatter
Males: Rich men are fatter than poor men.
Females: Rich women are thinner than poor women.
(*Brothers, p. 23*)

Rifle Shooting
Men and women perform equally well at rifle shooting, as strength is not a factor in performance.
(*Hammer, p. 21*)

Romantic
Men are more romantic than women.
(*Rubin, p. 56*)

Roofers
99.3 percent of roofers are male.
(*Hacker, p. 127*)

Runner's Knee
A woman is more susceptible to runner's knee due to her wider hips, which can cause the outer parts of her front thigh muscle to pull her kneecap to the side.
(*Selden, p. 53*)

Running
A woman's heels kick slightly sideways, rather than straight behind as a man's do.
(*Selden, p. 51*)

Running, Advantages Due to Sex
Males: Men can utilize oxygen more efficiently than women can, due to larger lungs, which enable them to run faster for short periods.

Females: Women have a lower metabolic rate and more fat on their bodies than men do, so they can endure running longer. A woman's lower weight is also an aid in running.

(*Shapescope,* Shape, *December 1981, p. 124*)

Running, Increase in Speed

Female: As of **1980**, women's running speeds have increased by an average of **28** percent since **1968**.

Male: Men's speeds have increased by only 0.3 percent.

(*Candance, p. 310*)

Women are now running about 90 percent as fast as men.

(*Dyer, p. 108*)

Running and Decreased Fertility

Low fertility has been shown to be a problem among serious runners of both sexes. Sperm count is low in some male runners, and some female runners experience amenorrhea (an absence of menstrual periods).

(*Mange, Johe, and Dayton, p. 261*)

Sales Demonstrators
96.7 percent of sales demonstrators are female.
(Hacker, p. 127)

Schizophrenia
Schizophrenia may occur at any age, but usually develops during early adulthood or adolescence. Usually, those affected with schizophrenia tend to withdraw from people, have feelings of grandeur or persecution, and a loss of a sense of reality. More women than men are diagnosed as schizophrenic.
(Cooley, p. 294)

Schizophrenia, Early Onset of
Upon hospital admission, more females than males are diagnosed "schizophrenia-early onset," which usually means that symptoms of the disease occurred in adolescence rather than in later adulthood.
(Franks and Burtle, p. 371)

Schizophrenia, Vulnerability to
Males: Males are most susceptible to schizophrenia during their twenties and thirties.
Females: Women are more vulnerable during pregnancy, childbirth, or menopause.
(About Schizophrenia, p. 8)

School Boards
Women comprise 37 percent of the members of school boards.
(*Zigli, front page*)

School District Administrators
In 1977, out of 16,000 school districts in the U.S.A., only 75 were administered by women.
(*Bird, p. 106, from the National Institute of Education*)

School Textbooks, Portrayal of the Sexes in Primary Grades
Males: Boys are pictured as active and in the out-of-doors.
Females: Girls are pictured as passive and inside the house.
(*Bird, p. 106, from the National Foundation for the Improvement of Education, 1977*)

Science, Doctoral Degrees Awarded in

	Biological Sciences	Physical and Mathematical Sciences
Males:	78%	88%
Females:	22%	12%

(*Yalow, p. 23*)

Scientists
In 1978, only 5.2 percent of the 2.74 million scientists in the U.S.A. were female.
(Graduate Woman, *September 1983, cover page*)

Scleroderma
(Scleroderma is a disease of the body's connective tissue. It is characterized by weakness, weight loss, fatigue, vague muscle pain, joint or bone pain, and unexplained swelling or thickening of the skin, for which there is no cure. There are about 300,000 victims of the disease in the United States.)

Women are approximately four times as likely to develop scleroderma during early and middle age as men are. The incidence rises with age, and in the later stages of life almost equal numbers of men and women are afflicted.
(Ha'ilono Kina, *December 1983, p. 8*)

Scoliosis (Curvature of the Spine)
Ninety percent of those afflicted with scoliosis are female. The causes are unknown, but are thought to be related to hormonal imbalances.

(SerVaas, p. 62; Harvard Medical School Healthletter, March 1981, p. 6)

Secondary Achievement Tests (SAT) Scores, Averages (1981)
Minimum score is 200, maximum score is 800.

Verbal: *Male*—428
Female—420
Math: *Male*—491
Female—443

(Census, p. 151)

Secretaries
99.2 percent of secretaries are female.

(Bureau of Labor Statistics, 1981)

Secretary of State
All Secretaries of State of the United States have been male.

(Almanac, p. 282)

Secretary of the Treasury
All Secretaries of the Treasury of the United States have been men.

(Almanac, 1981, p. 283)

Sedatives, Prescribed by a Physician
Males: Twelve million men have utilized sedatives prescribed by a physician.
Females: Sixteen million women have utilized sedatives prescribed by a physician.

(Levy, p. 196)

Selenium
Selenium is a mineral found in eggs, tuna, broccoli, bran, and wheat germ.
Male: Men have a greater need for selenium than women do, for it is lost in the semen. One half of a man's supply is in the genital area so it may influence genital health.

Female: Selenium has been helpful to some women in decreasing hot flashes during menopause.

(*Mindell, p. 114*)

Senators, U.S.

There have been 1,726 senators elected since 1776. Eleven of them have been women.

(*Bird, p. 109*)

Only two of the hundred U.S. senators are female.

(*Time, 7/12/82, p. 20*)

Senile Brain Syndrome

(Senility is a brain disorder that rarely occurs before age seventy. Onset is gradual and may involve impaired intellectual functions such as memory, and orientation in time and place. The senile may become quarrelsome, irritable, have irrational thoughts, refuse to eat or have temper tantrums.)

Senility is found more often in women than in men.

(*Cooley, p. 294*)

Sensitivity, Emotional

Women are more emotionally sensitive than men.

(*Ford, p. 110*)

Sensitivity to Stimuli

Women are more sensitive to visual sound and touch stimuli than men are.

(*Goleman, p. 59*)

Separation from One's Spouse, Fears of

Males: Men fear they will not be able to find another woman, will be lonely or depressed, and worry about losing the comforts of marriage.

Females: Women fear it will be dangerous to be without their husbands.

(*Gould, p. 54*)

Sergeants

Of 689,965 sergeants in the armed forces, 29,412 are women.

(*Hacker, p. 206*)

Sewers and Stitchers
In 1980, 95.7 percent of sewers and stitchers were female.
(Hacker, p. 128)

Sex, Casual
Women display much less interest in casual sex than men do.
(Collier, p. 84)

Sex: Good or Bad?
Male: If sexual attraction is present, then sex can be good. A positive relationship is not necessary for men to enjoy sex.
Female: If the relationship is positive, then sex is good. Without a positive relationship, sex for a woman is usually not good.
(Hagen, p. 155)

Sex, Teenagers' Views Regarding Discussing with Parents
Males: Sixty-six percent of the teenage males surveyed said they would not talk openly with their parents about sex.
Females: Sixty-five percent of the teenage females said they would not talk openly about sex with their parents.

(The reasons given related to the perception on the part of the teenagers that the parents might be shocked or angry.)
(From a study on teenage sexuality by Hass, in Parade Magazine, *by Shearer, 1/13/83)*

Sex, Why Not?
Male: "I could not talk her into it."
Female: "I did not love the person."
(Hagen, p. 157)

Sex Differences and the Division of Labor
Divisions of labor and variations in the behavior acceptable for members of each sex exist in every culture. However, with the exception of those behaviors involving reproduction and lactation, what is considered "masculine" and what "feminine" differs from society to society.
(Lowe and Hubhard, p. 99)

Sex Discrimination and Looking for a Job
Both men and women suffer from sex discrimination in looking

for jobs. Male applicants have a harder time trying to obtain a traditionally female job than do women seeking a traditionally male job.

(*Researcher: Richard Levinson in Horn,* Psychology Today, *March 1975, p. 21*)

Sex Drive and Neurotransmitters

Neurotransmitters are chemical messages that send signals to various parts of the body. In the case of the sex drive, it is felt that the neurotransmitter, serotonin, is utilized to increase the woman's drive. Thus, carbohydrates, which encourage production of this chemical, are thought to be beneficial to the woman with a low sex drive. As norepinephrine, which is stimulated by protein, plays a major role in the sex drive of the male, a high protein diet might help to increase his drive.

(*Morgan, p. 22*)

Sexes, Ratios of, by Age

For every 100 men between ages 15–34, there are 123 women.
For every 100 men between ages 35–39, there are 124 women.
For every 100 men between ages 40–44, there are 128 women.
For every 100 men between ages 45–54, there are 159 women.

(*Foreman, p. C1*)

Sex Life of People over 60

Women over sixty do not have as active a sex life as men over sixty, due to a shortage of male partners. At age sixty, 94 percent of men, but only 80 percent of women, are still active sexually.

(*Mitchell, p. 168; Collier, p. 84*)

Sex Roles, as Presented in Grade School and Preschool Stories

Females are not represented as often as males, and when they are, they play insignificant roles, with women baking or doing chores. In contrast, males are presented as leading adventurous, exciting lives.

(*Franks and Burtle, p. 333*)

Sex Roles, Traditional Views

Male: A man is seen as protecting the female because he is physically stronger. He initiates and makes the major decisions. He is seen as the breadwinner.

Female: A woman is seen as the caretaker of the home and children, and as one who cares for and defers to others.
  (*Gilligan, p. 68; Ford, pp. 104–114; Adams, p. 54*)

Sexual Abuse, Mean Age of Victimized Children
Males: The mean age of the males suffering sexual abuse is eleven.
Females: The mean age of females suffering sexual abuse is ten.
  (*Finkelhor, p. 7*)

Sexual Activity after 40
Male: Testicular secretion declines after age forty, which accounts for the reduction in sexual activity among older men.
Female: Sexual activity declines somewhat for women after its peak in the mid-thirties.
  (*Wagenvoord/Bailey, Men, p. 151*)

Sexual Activity and Energy
Various reports indicate that sexual activity, hormonal levels, and energy are linked in some manner. The following information may shed light on the matter:
Males: Men who are sexually active have increased levels of testosterone.
Females: Women who are sexually active have increased levels of progesterone, the hormone that helps release energy. They also have increased levels of testosterone, which is important in the utilization of proteins.
  (*Haines and Tyson, in* Everywoman, *November 1981, p. 58*)

Sexual Desire and Hormonal Influence
Both females and males derive their sexual appetites from the hormone testosterone. Both have different quantities of the hormone in their systems at different times of their lives. In a male, testosterone levels are quite high at about age twenty—usually the time of peak sexual desire. In the female, the level of testosterone begins to rise between thirty and thirty-five. At menopause, the levels of this hormone are higher in women, and, in a man of sixty, can be as low as that of a ten-year-old boy.
  (*Gross, p. 207; Hagen, p. 130; Mitchell, p. 39; Woman's Body, p. 43*)

Sexual Desire and the Seasons
Males: Sexual activity seems to peak in September. (Testosterone levels generally peak in September.)
Females: Sexual activity often peaks in July and tapers off in September.
(*Glassman, p. 76*)

Sexual Deviants
Five to 10 percent of the population is sexually deviant. The majority are men.
(*Kolb, pp. 503–507*)

Sexual Dysfunctions
Males: One third of the males interviewed indicated they had had a sexual dysfunction at one time in their lives.
Females: One fourth of the women interviewed indicated they had had a sexual dysfunction at some time in their lives.
(*Redbook, 1981, p. 140*)

Sexual Dysfunction, Reactions to
Males: Men develop symptoms of depression and anxiety when either they or their partner is sexually dysfunctional.
Females: Women whose husbands or lovers are dysfunctional in some way do not develop any symptoms. Women who are considered dysfunctional (have some sexual difficulty) do manifest anxiety.
(*Researchers: Leonard Derogatis, Ph.D., and Bridget Gallant, Johns Hopkins School of Medicine*)

Sexual Functions, Primary
Males: "Men ejaculate."
Females: "Women menstruate, gestate, and lactate."
(*Newsweek, 5/18/81, p. 73*)

Sexual Harassment
In one study, men complained of being harassed sexually by both men and women. In 28 percent of the cases, it was by male employees. Forty-two percent of the women surveyed complained of being harassed sexually by male bosses and fellow employees.
(*Star, 6/21/83, p. 19*)

Sexual Harassment in the Civil Service

(Sexual harassment was defined in a study by the Merit System Protection Board as actual or attempted rape, pressure for sexual behaviors, leaning over, leering, cornering, and pinching.)

Male: Fifteen percent of the men in government service had experienced sexual harassment.

Female: Forty-two percent of the women had experienced sexual harassment.

Women were most likely to be sexually harassed in the Department of Labor, and men in the Health and Human Services Department and the Veterans Administration. Fifty-five percent of women in the Department of Labor had been approached, and 22 percent of men in Health and Human Services and the VA had been approached.

(Hacker, p. 202)

Sexual Integration in the Navy

Men and women in the navy perform equally well in terms of ease, expertise, and dedication.

(Adams, p. 53)

Sexual Intercourse, Complaints of Infrequency

More women than men complain of infrequent lovemaking.

(Researcher: Robert Putnam, Director for the Society for the Scientific Study of Sex; Murray, p. 263)

Sexual Intercourse, Compulsive Need for

The compulsive need to have recurrent sexual intercourse with different partners, without falling in love and without being paid, is called "nymphomania" in females and "satyriasis" in males.

(Money, pp. 221 and 223)

Sexual Organs, Location of

Male: The male sexual organs are located outside the body and are relatively vulnerable.

Female: The female reproductive organs are safely imbedded in the pelvic region.

(Selden, p. 53)

Sexual Peak, Age Differences
Male: Men seem to experience the greatest sexual desire in their late teens and early twenties.
Female: Women's greatest sexual desire seems to occur in their thirties.
(Woman's Body, p. 43; Gross, p. 207)

Sexual Preference in Parents for Their Firstborn
Both usually prefer a male child.
(Brothers, p. 39)

Sexual Problems Most Commonly Discussed with Physicians
Males: Premature ejaculation and sexual impotence are the male problems most frequently discussed with a physician.
Females: Failure to achieve orgasm is probably the most common female sexual problem discussed with a physician.
(Flowers/Abram, p. 227)

Sexual Relations with a Stranger for One Million Dollars
Male: Seventy-eight percent of the men surveyed said they would consent to sexual intercourse with a stranger in return for a million dollars.
Female: Fifty-eight percent of the women surveyed said they would consent.
(Psychology Today Survey, May 1981, p. 29)

Sexual Response, After "The Change of Life"
Male: Although testosterone levels and, consequently, sexual drive, declines among men over age forty, sexual activity is possible, desirable, and encouraged for any man at any age. (Hawaiian men say that as long as they can perform sexually, they are not old men.)
Female: Twenty percent of the women surveyed reported that sexual desire increased after menopause. Sixty percent said their feelings were unchanged.
(Woman's Body, p. 189)

Sexual Response, Excitement Stage
During this stage the genitals of both sexes are congested with blood, and the nipples of both are erect.

Males: Testes begin their elevation into the body and there is penile erection.
Females: Lubrication of the vagina occurs as does a lengthening and swelling of the vagina.
(Woman's Body, *p. 29*)

Sexual Response, Orgasmic Stage
Orgasm lasts for only a few seconds, as congestion, blood pressure, heart rate, breathing, and muscular tension reach a peak and return to normal in both sexes.
Males: In the male, ejaculation of the semen into the vagina occurs.
Females: There is great variation among females in the duration and intensity of the experience.
(*Masters and Johnson, p. 299*)

Sexual Response, Plateau Stage
In both sexes, the following occurs during the plateau stage of sexual response: blood pressure elevates, hyperventilation occurs, the heart beats rapidly, and genital lubrication takes place.
Males: In the male, the circumference of the penis increases, the penis becomes fully elevated, and the head of the penis may redden.
Females: In the female, the clitoris retracts, the labia minoria reddens, the vaginal opening narrows, and the uterus elevates.
(*Masters and Johnson, pp. 280–81*)

Sexual Response, Resolution Stage
Males: During the resolution stage, men cannot be restimulated to a higher level of sexual tension, as can women.
Females: During this phase, women may experience a series of orgasms.
(*Wagenvoord/Bailey, Women, pp. 134, 135*)

Sheetmetal Workers
96.9 percent of sheetmetal workers are male.
(*Hacker, p. 127*)

"Shooting the Wall" (Some call it "hitting the wall")
(A term used by runners to describe sudden pain and weakness

experienced after running for a certain length of time.)
Male: Male runners often report "shooting the wall" after running for two hours, the point at which glycogen (which fuels their muscles) is depleted.
Female: Few women report "hitting the wall." Experts feel their extra fat gives them an endurance men don't have. (The fat can be converted to energy and the women can continue to run.) Or it may be due to increased hormone secretions, stimulated by the exercise.
   (Eastman, p. 96)

Shoulders
Male: The male shoulders are stonger and broader than the female's, maximizing the capacity to hit and throw.
Female: Women have narrower shoulders than men, enabling them to cut through water more easily, an aid in swimming.
   (Selden, p. 53)

Shy
Women are no shyer than men.
   (Zimbardo, Norwood, Pilkonis, p. 72)

Singing
More women than men can sing in tune.
   (Goleman, p. 49)

Singles
Male: In 1981, 38.3 percent of those living alone were men.
Female: 61.7 percent of those living alone were women. There were about 6 million singles in America in 1981, and their numbers are expected to rise in the future.
   (Sanoff, p. 54)

Size
Men are about 10 percent bigger than women.
   (Wagenvoord/Bailey, Women, p. 95)

Skeletal Muscles
Members of both sexes have some four hundred skeletal muscles.
   (Wagenvoord/Bailey, Men, p. 70)

Skeletal Structural Differences
Male: Men have wider shoulders, longer arms and legs, heavier bones, and larger joints than women.
Female: Women have wider hips, more flexible joints, and arms that angle slightly.
> *(Wagenvoord/Bailey, Men, p. 61)*

Skiing, Falls
Males: Men tend to fall on their faces.
Females: Women tend to fall on their backs, as the woman's center of gravity is lower.
> *(Selden, p. 53)*

Skin
The skin is the largest organ in the body of either sex.
Male: In the male the skin covers an area of about twenty square feet, and is thicker than that of the female.
Female: A female's skin covers an area of about seventeen and a half square feet, and is thinner than that of the male.
> *(Wagenvoord/Bailey, Men, p. 74)*

Skin and Aging
Male: A man's skin ages about ten years more slowly than that of the female.
Female: Lacking the oils found in a man's skin, a woman's skin ages more rapidly.
> *(Brothers, p. 5)*

Skin and Wrinkles
The thickness of a man's skin prevents the sun's radiation from penetrating and damaging it. A woman's thinner skin provides less protection, which is why she has more wrinkles than he does.
> *(Brothers, Woman's Day, 2/9/82, p. 138)*

Skull
A woman's skull is thinner than a man's, and smaller at the base, but greater in circumference at the crown.
> *(Wagenvoord/Bailey, Women, p. 64)*

Sleepers, "Sneak"
Sneak sleepers are those who doze off for two to fifteen seconds, usually while they are sitting up. Men are more likely to sneak sleep than women are.
(*"Parade Hotline,"* Parade Magazine, 6/29/80, p. 24)

Sleeping and Restlessness
Restless sleeping occurs more often in boys than in girls, up to age eleven. At age fourteen restless sleeping disappears entirely for girls, and is reduced in boys.
(*Simonds and Parraga,* p. 387)

Sleeping Pills (1976)
Male: 4.5 million men use sleeping pills.
Female: 9.4 million women use sleeping pills.
(Statistical Abstract, p. 123)

Small Business
Women own over one fourth of the 15 million small businesses, but earn only 9 percent of the small business revenues.
(*"Let's Put Our Heads Together,"* p. 19)

Smiling
Women smile more than men.
(Human Behavior, *June 1977,* p. 32)

Smiling in Infants
Girl babies smile more often than boy babies.
(*Wagenvoord/Bailey,* Women, p. 16)

Smokeout, Great American
The American Cancer Society reports that a telephone survey of 2,123 households indicated that 29 percent of the male smokers and 43.7 percent of the female smokers were attempting to complete the twenty-four-hour nicotine fast during the Great American Smokeout in 1983.
(*Honolulu* Advertiser, 11/18/83, p. A29)

Smoking
Men smoke more than women.
(Geosphere, *August 1981,* p. 142)

Smoking, Quitting
More men than women have quit smoking.
(Geosphere, *August 1981, p. 142*)

Snacking
Males: 40.1 percent of men snack daily.
Females: 36.3 percent of women snack daily.
(Statistical Abstract of the U.S.A., *1982–83, p. 125*)

Snoring
Men snore more than women.
(*Brothers, p. 5*)

Social Cues
Girl babies are more responsive to social cues than boy babies are.
(Newsweek, *5/18/81, p. 73*)

Social Interests as Children
Both sexes are socially inclined. Boys seem to like to be with larger groups of other boys, whereas girls prefer to be with either one friend or with a small group.
(*Wagenvoord/Bailey*, Men, *p. 26; Mitchell, pp. 93, 94*)

Social Lives
Women experience less exciting and interesting social lives than men.
(*Verbrugge*, Parade Magazine, *11/14/82*)

Socially Responsive
Women are more socially responsive than men. From the cradle on, girl infants smile more, prefer a face to a toy, and vocalize more. Women are better at reading nonverbal cues and body language than men are, and are more sensitive to facial cues.
(*Goleman, p. 59; Hammer, p. 26*)

Social Sciences, Doctorates
Male: In the 1979–80 academic year, 65.4 percent of the doctorates in social sciences were awarded to men.
Female: 34.6 percent were awarded to women.
(*Hacker, p. 244*)

Social Security Benefits, Average
Male: In 1981, average yearly social security benefits for men were $4,880.
Female: The average yearly social security benefits for women were $3,403.
    (Hacker, p. 184)

Social Work, Performance in Schools of
Women perform better than men in schools of social work, making better grades both academically and in field work. Women in social work also have higher undergraduate grades than their male counterparts, and more women than men finish or enter doctoral programs in social work.
    (Kirk and Rosenblatt, p. 437)

Social Work Administrators
Men hold the "top" positions in social work even though the majority of social workers are female.
    (Kirk and Rosenblatt, p. 25)

Social Workers
Males: One third of social workers are men.
Females: Two thirds of social workers are women.
    (Kirk and Rosenblatt, p. 431)

Spatial Ability
Males are superior at tasks involving spatial ability, according to numerous studies. Such abilities are useful for manipulating objects and communicating about them, such as reading a map, putting a computer together, or building a bridge.
    (Goleman, p. 59)

Spatial Ability, Development of
The right hemisphere of a boy's brain (the spatial side) becomes specialized by age six, whereas the same development can take up to age thirteen in a girl.
    (Researcher: Sandra Wittleson, Ph.D., McMaster University, Ontario; Wagenvoord/Bailey, Women, p. 24)

Spatial Tests
Twenty-five percent of women do as well as 75 percent of men in spatial tests such as mazes, picture completion, and map reading.
(*Researcher: Philip Bryden, Ph.D., University of Waterloo in Ontario*)

Speaking
Girls learn to speak earlier than boys and surpass them in speech abilities at age eleven or so.
(Newsweek, 5/18/81, p. 73)

Speaking, Public
In a survey of two hundred people, it was found that 50 percent of the women and 20 percent of the men were unable to speak in public.
(*Dowling, p. 50*)

Speech Center in the Brain and Maturity
The speech center in the left hemisphere of the brain matures more rapidly in girls than in boys.
(*Researcher: Doreen Kimura, Ph.D., University of Southern Ontario; Wagenvoord/Bailey, Men, p. 25*)

Speech Defects
Females are less likely than males to have speech defects.
(*Arkoff, p. 64*)

Speech Style
Women are more indirect, polite, and gentle in their speech than men are.
(*Bellinger and Gleason, p. 1123*)

Spelling
Girls excel at spelling.
(Newsweek, 5/18/81, p. 73)

Sperm and Ova, Life Span of
Male: Sperm cells are developed inside the testes of a man at the rate of approximately 200 million per day. It takes from sixty to seventy-two days for an individual sperm cell to mature. Once

intercourse has occurred, a sperm cell can live in the top of the fallopian tube for up to seventy-two hours, as conditions there are favorable for its survival.

Female: Normally one mature egg is produced in a woman each month. If it is not fertilized within twenty-four to forty-eight hours after it gets to the fallopian tube, it will begin to degenerate.

(Woman's Body, *pp. 88, 89*)

Sports Abilities

Men still rank first in most sports, but the training that women athletes are currently undergoing has many authorities wondering if male and female athletes will indeed be of equal abilities in the future.

(Newsweek, *5/18/81, p. 75*)

Spouse, Attractive, and Perception of Others

Male: Homely men with attractive wives are seen as smart and successful breadwinners.

Female: A homely wife with an attractive husband is seen as marrying "above herself."

(Researcher: *Daniel Bar-Tel, Tel Aviv University, Israel, and Leonora Saxes, Boston University;* Human Behavior, *April 1977, p. 37*)

Spouse Abuse

1.8 million wives are beaten by their husbands each year. One in ten female partners experience some degree of spouse violence within a year.

(Schuman, *p. 69*)

Sprinting

Men do better at sprinting because they have more stored fuel and more muscle.

(Selden, *p. 96*)

Standard of Living after a Divorce

A man's standard of living usually rises after a divorce, while for a woman with children it usually lowers, unless she remarries (then it goes higher than it was with husband Number One.)

(Jencks, *p. 73*)

Staphylococcus Infections
More men than women are afflicted by staph.
  (Brothers, Woman's Day, 2/9/82, p. 138)

State Boards, Appointed Positions
Males: In 1979 men held 85 percent of the appointed positions on state boards.
Females: Women held 15 percent of all appointed positions on state boards.
  (Bird, p. 112)

State Legislators
Women make up 12 percent of state legislative bodies.
  (Avery, p. 88)

Stealing for a Million Dollars
More men than women said they would steal if they were given a million dollars.
  (Psychology Today Survey, May 1981, p. 29)

Sterilization
About the same numbers of husbands and wives are sterilized.
  (Horn, February 1978, p. 43)

Sterilization as the Most Popular Form of Birth Control
Sterilization is the most popular form of birth control for couples married ten years or more, and is on equal status with the pill for all married couples.
  (Horn, February 1978, p. 43)

Stillbirths
There are more male than female stillbirths.
  (Man's Body, pp. A01–02)

Stonemasons
99.9 percent of stone masons are male.
  (Hacker, p. 127)

Stories for Children, Roles in
Males: Men occupy exciting positions in children's stories and

are pictured in over one hundred fifty roles.
Females: Women take second place to men in children's stories,
and occupy traditional roles such as those of housewife, teacher,
and secretary.

(*Bird, p. 106*)

Strength
The female has two thirds the overall strength of the male.

(*Billies, p. 115*)

Strength, Abdominal
Men and women are equal in terms of abdominal strength.

(*Brothers, p. 23*)

Strength, Physical
The average woman has only one third the strength of a man in
the upper part of her body and only two thirds the man's
strength in her legs. Only her stomach muscles are as strong as
his. Most feel the woman has only one half the total strength of a
man.

(*Selden, July 1981, pp. 51, 53*)

Strength and Power
Men have more massive bones, larger joints, and longer arms and
leg segments, which give them greater leverage. (Some authorities feel that, with training, women may catch up to men.)

(*Newsweek, 5/18/81, p. 75*)

Stress
Women report more stress than men. Most authorities feel this is
because women work and also have the responsibility of caring
for their husbands and children. Many people also seem to feel
that a man's work is always more important than a woman's, and
that this priority adds further to her stress. (As the world begins
to understand that the economy demands that women work, per-
haps her work and her income will be viewed as just as important as those of a man.)

(*Rubinstein, p. 32*)

Men experience more stress than women. (This is an area that
some feel is changing rapidly.)

(*Newsweek, 5/18/81, p. 74*)

Stress, Handling of
As women are more sensitive to stimuli, they may be unable to handle heavy stress as well as men can.

(Psychology Today, *November 1978, p. 48*)

Stress and Chemical Secretion
Women release less adrenaline than men do under stress. They also cry more, releasing more prolactin and leucine-enkephalin (neurotransmitters that are related to pain relief and emotional stress).

(Health, *p. 22; Kotulak, p. A13*)

Stress and Infertility
Male: Stress can cause muscle spasms in the sperm ducts and thus interfere with the transmission of semen.

Female: Stress can cause an enlarged uterus, can prevent ovulation, and can cause abnormal cervical secretions that immobilize sperm. It can also disturb uterine blood circulation enough to detach the placenta, and lead to spontaneous abortion.

(Cory, Psychology Today, *March 1980, pp. 33, 34*)

Stress and Its Effect on Sexual Glands
Male: Stress can impede sexual hormone production and sperm production. Men under stress usually have a diminished sex drive and may ejaculate prematurely.

Female: Stress may cause heavy menstrual periods in women and can reduce the flow of milk in nursing mothers.

(Woman's Body, *p. 352; LaMott, p. 51*)

Stress and Marriage
More wives than husbands report marital stress. They show less desire to save their marriage and they report problems in more than twice as many areas as do husbands. Also, more wives than husbands have considered separation or divorce, or have regretted their marriages.

(Bernard, *pp. 28, 29*)

Stress from Work, Handling of
Exercise is the most popular method of dealing with work-related stress, for both sexes. The second most popular methods

are eating, daydreaming, or buying something. Women are more likely than men to utilize all four methods. Women are also quicker to seek counseling for stress.

(*Renwick, Lawler, and the* Psychology Today *staff, p. 60*)

Stroke
(A stroke results from failure of the blood to reach a part of the brain.)

A man is more likely to suffer a stroke than a woman is.

(Man's Body, *pp. B25–27*)

Stroke, Damage from
Males are more likely than females to suffer speech impairment after damage to the left hemisphere of the brain, or the loss of such nonverbal functions as visual or spatial ability.

(*Brothers,* Woman's Day, *2/9/82, p. 142; Murphy, p. 49*)

Stroke, Recovery from
Women do better in verbal and spatial testing after a stroke than men do. They tend to be less disabled and to recover more quickly.

(*Brothers,* Woman's Day, *2/9/82; Murphy, p. 49*)

Stroke Volume
The amount of blood the heart pumps per beat is called stroke volume, and is regulated by the amount of oxygen in the blood. Men have more oxygen-carrying hemoglobin in the blood and therefore have larger stroke volumes. As muscles depend on oxygen to work, men are able to excel at running and aerobic activities because of their large stroke volume.

(*Hammer, p. 21*)

Stuttering
Male stutterers outnumber female by five to one.

(Newsweek, *5/18/81, p. 73*)

Success, Fear of in Athletics
Women are more fearful of success in sports than are men. "Fear of success" is a common theme running through the literature on male and female differences.

(*Silva, p. 94*)

(See *The Cinderella Complex* by Colette Dowling for a delightful explanation of this fear in females.)

Success or Failure, Beliefs about
In the course of research on people's beliefs as to why men and women succeed or fail, by Sara Kiesler, Shirley Feldman-Summers and Kay Deaux, the following attitudes toward success and failure were noted:

(1) Both sexes tend to attribute male success to competence, and female success to hard work and luck.

(2) When a man fails, both men and women believe it is because he has been unlucky. If a woman does poorly, it is because she isn't very competent.

(*Norman, p. 70; Deaux, p. 70*)

Suggestibility
No sex differences noted.

(*Parlee, p. 69*)

Suicide
26,832 suicides were recorded in 1979.
Male: 72.6 percent, or 19,493 of the victims, were men.
Female: 27.4 percent, or 7,339, were women.

(*Hacker, p. 73*)

Suicide Among Young Physicians
Young women physicians are more likely to commit suicide than are male physicians of the same age.

(*Kirk and Rosenblatt, p. 438*)

Suicide and Age
Male: The suicide rate for men is highest among those between seventy-five and eighty-four years of age.
Female: The suicide rate for women is highest among those in middle age.

(*Man's Body, pp. B60–62*)

Suicide Attempts
Male: Three of four male suicide attempts will be successful.
Female: Suicide attempts are high among young women; how-

ever, of four women who attempt it, only one succeeds.
(Man's Body, *pp. B60–62*)

Suicide Methods
Male: Men favor shooting and hanging as methods of killing themlselves.
Female: Women favor slow-acting poisons and barbiturates.
(Man's Body, *p. B62*)

Suicide Rate After an Unhappy Love Affair
The number of men who commit suicide after an unhappy love affair is three times that of the number of women who do so.
(Z. Rubin, Human Behavior, *February 1977, p. 56*)

Superiority, Biological
Women live longer, and have fewer diseases and lower suicide rates than men. They are better at producing antibodies, have a lower incidence of viral and bacterial diseases, fewer accidents, and outlive men by an average of about eight years.
(Science Digest, *September 1982, p. 90*)

Superstitiousness
Women are said to be more superstitious than men, especially about walking under a ladder, putting a hat on the bed, black cats, and Friday the 13th.
(Eppingham, *p. 37*)

Surgery
Of ten patients who undergo surgery, six are women. Half of the ten operations most frequently performed are performed solely on women.
(Star, *6/21/83, p. 19*)

Surgery and Risk
Surgery is riskier for men, as females are able to produce blood more easily and faster than men can, although a man's blood does clot faster than a woman's.
(Brothers, Woman's Day, *2/9/82, p. 139; Foley, p. 59*)

Surveyors
96.6 percent of surveyors are male.
  (*Hacker, p. 127*)

Sweet Foods
Males prefer very sweet foods more than females do.
  (Psychology Today, *1978, p. 106*)

Swimming
Women excel at swimming. They have more fat and therefore more buoyancy. Fat stored in the upper legs improves streamlining in the water. They also use 30 percent less energy than men when swimming.
  (Newsweek, *5/18/81, p. 75*)

Symphony Managers (Major Orchestras)
Males: 96 percent of the managers of major symphony orchestras are men.
Females: 4 percent are women.
  (*Bird, p. 88*)

Symptoms of Illness
More women than men report symptoms of illness and do more to alleviate the symptoms.
  (*Verbrugge*, Parade Magazine, *11/12/82*)

Syphilis Rates
(Syphilis, a very serious venereal disease, is the third most common disease reported. It is caused by tiny bacteria shaped like corkscrews that thrive in the warmth of the genital passages and the rectum, and is usually contracted through physical contact. Antibiotics are used to treat the disease, which usually appears about three weeks after contact. Early symptoms include sores and swelling in the groin area. If the disease is not treated in the early stages, it can cause insanity or can blind, paralyze, cripple, or kill the victim.)

The highest rates, among both men and women, are in the ages between twenty and twenty-four. Men have higher rates than women. There are 5,605 syphilis cases per 100,000 for men, and 2,027 per 100,000 for women in that age range. In 1980 the total number of cases in men was 20,767; the total in women was 6,437.

(Woman's Body, *pp. 372, 373; Hacker, p. 79*)

Tactile Sensitivity (Sensitivity to Touch)
Women have superior tactile sensitivity, even in infancy.
(Newsweek, 5/18/81, p. 73)

Tailors
One half of all tailors are female.
(Murphy, p. 51)

Talk
Men talk about themselves much less than women do.
(Human Behavior, January 1979, p. 34)

Target Heart Rate
(How fast your pulse can go, safely, for maximum aerobic benefits.)
Male: Subtract your age from 220, then multiply by 75 percent to determine your maximum safe pulse rate per minute.
Female: Subtract your age from 226, then multiply by 75 percent.
(Luna, p. 26)

Teacher Expectations
Teachers expect boys to be self-reliant and physically aggressive, and girls to be dependent and passive.
(Serbin and O'Leary, p. 57)

Teachers
In 1983, 90 percent of teachers were female.
(Murphy, p. 50)

Teachers, Elementary
In 1983, 80 percent of all elementary teachers were female.
(Murphy, p. 50)

Teachers, High School
In 1981, half the teachers in secondary or high schools were male.
(Safran, p. 12)

Teachers, Kindergarten
In 1981, of 48,000 kindergarten teachers, only 1 percent was male.
(Murphy, p. 50)

Teachers, National Teacher Awards, 1966–81
Male: Men have won the National Teacher Award six times.
Female: Women have won nine times.
(Almanac, 1981, p. 403)

Teachers' Sex Biases
From nursery school through graduate schools, teachers call on male students more than on female students. Females are called on much less in math and science, since males are assumed to be better in these subjects. Studies have shown that the students who are active in class are the ones who go on to higher achievement.
(Safran, p. 12)

Teaching, Hands-on Instruction
Boys receive more hands-on instruction—in which one shows a person how to do something by doing it oneself—from their instructors than do girls. They are twice as likely as girls to receive individual instruction from a teacher. They also receive more verbal rewards for academic pursuits.
(Serbin and O'Leary, p. 102)

Technical and Vocational Educational Programs
Male: In 1983, 82 percent of the students in technical and vocational programs were men.
Female: 18 percent of the students enrolled in technical and vocational school programs were women.
    (*Caudle, p. 8*)

Telephone Conversations
60 percent of all nonbusiness telephone calls are made by women.
    (*Murphy, p. 51*)

Telephone Operators
91.8 percent of telephone operators are female.
    (*Hacker, p. 128*)

Television, Advertisement of Health Products
More women than men are shown on TV commercials as needing medication.
    (*Brothers*, Woman's Day, *2/9/82, p. 138*)

Television, Hiring for Children's Programs
Only one woman for every two men is hired for children's television shows.
    (*Bird, p. 88*)

Television Jobs
For every seventy actors hired for television jobs, thirty actresses will be hired.
    (*Bird, p. 88; Actors' Guild Study*)

Television Viewers
73.6 million people watch television daily. Of these, 54 percent are female.
    (*Clarke, p. 12*)

Temperature
A woman's average body temperature is slightly lower than a man's.
    (*Selden, p. 52*)

Temperature, Genital Requirements
Male: Testicles do not function well at high temperatures (which is why they hang outside the body), and sperm production may be curtailed when the testicles are kept warm for prolonged periods (such as in a bath or hot tub).
Female: The female genital and reproductive system is concealed internally, as the ovaries require warmth for efficient egg production.
(*Hyman, p. 298*)

Temperature Sensitivity
Men are less sensitive to extreme heat, and more sensitive to extreme cold, than women are.
(*Selden, p. 52*)

Tenure, Colleges
Women hold 16.5 percent of the tenured positions at four-year colleges.
(*Horn, September 1978, p. 78*)

Testosterone
(A sex hormone, testosterone is found in both males and females.)
Males: Produced by the testes, this hormone is responsible for secondary sex characteristics. It increases the likelihood of high blood pressure in men, increases the weight of muscle tissue, and enlarges the muscle fibers. Testosterone seems to increase the likelihood of heart attacks if given to either men or women. It rises both during fights and with sexual desire. Although the levels fall and rise during the day, a man can have as much as ten to fifteen times as much testosterone as a woman.

After age forty, a man's testosterone level gradually diminishes until, at age sixty, it is about that of a nine-year-old (though sexual function is still intact in a healthy sixty-year-old male).
Females: Testosterone is produced by the adrenal glands in women and is responsible for sex drive. It increases after menopause.
(*Riddle, p. 23; Brothers, p. 11; S. Hammer, p. 22; Money, p. 207;* Woman's Body, *p. 396*)

Testosterone Levels and Aggression
Members of both sexes are more aggressive when testosterone levels are high. In females this occurs at menstruation, when the levels of estrogen and progesterone are low. In contrast, during midcycle when levels of testosterone and estrogen are high, women have feelings of well-being, assertiveness, and self-esteem.
> *(Franks and Burtle, p.35, 43)*

Testosterone Supplements, Side Effects
Male: When men take natural supplements of testosterone they may become more aggressive, cease producing the hormone within their own bodies, their sperm counts may drop, their testicles may shrink, and breasts may develop. When synthetic testosterone is taken, liver damage, liver tumors, hypertension, and atherosclerosis may occur.
Female: In women, natural or synthetic testosterone may cause an increase in aggression, temporary infertility, or acne. Women may begin to go bald or grow beards. Synthetic testosterone may also cause destruction of the liver and arteries.
> *(Angier, pp. 98, 100, 101)*

Theology Degrees Awarded
Male: 85.6 percent of the theology degrees awarded in the 1979–80 academic year were awarded to men.
Female: 14.4 percent went to women.
> *(Hacker, p. 244)*

Therapist, Preferences for
Male: The majority of men prefer a male therapist.
Female: The majority of women prefer a male therapist.
> *(Franks and Burtle, p. 86)*

Therapy, Most Commonly Reported Problem
Lack of sexual desire on the part of either the male or the female is the most common problem reported to a therapist.
> *(Redbook, February 1981, p. 142)*

Thigh Muscles
A woman's strongest muscles are her thigh muscles, which, if

exercised vigorously, can develop up to 85 percent of the strength of a man's thigh muscles.
(*Dyer, p. 109*)

Three-dimensional Perception
Males succeed more than females in tests involving three-dimensional perception.
(*Goleman, p. 59*)

Throwing
Men excel in throwing due to stronger and broader shoulders.
(*Selden, p. 53*)

Throwing a Ball
Male: Men prefer to throw overhand, as their arms form a straight line; they can exert more pressure in this manner and throw the ball farther.
(Man's Body, *pp. A10–12*)
Female: Women usually prefer to throw underhand because of the way in which their arms angle out from their bodies.
(Man's Body, *p. 61*)

Thumbs
A woman's thumbs are considerably weaker and smaller than a man's.
(*Wagenvoord/Bailey,* Women, *p. 64*)

Tight Jeans and No Bra Worn by a Woman, Meaning of to Both Sexes
Male: She wants to have sex.
Female: She is in style.
(*Cory, 10/80, p. 24*)

Tippers, Business People
Male: Businessmen tip at a rate of between 10 percent to 15 percent.
Female: Businesswomen tip at a rate of about 20 percent.
(*"Fiddle, Faddle, Fun and Fury,"* New Woman, *July-August 1980, p. 12*)

Tool and Die Makers
97.2 percent of tool and die makers are male.
(*Hacker, p. 127*)

Touching and Sexual Arousal
Both sexes respond equally to touching.
(*Wagenvoord/Bailey*, Men, *pp. 148, 149*)

Tourette Syndrome
Tourette syndrome is a neurological disorder characterized by involuntary muscular movements, uncontrollable vocal sounds, and verbal outbursts. Considered a rare disorder, it is most common in male children between the ages of two to fifteen. There are about 3.5 million people affected by the disease worldwide, and neurologists estimate that there may be as many as 100,000 undiagnosed cases in the U.S.A. Although this condition is chronic, it is not a degenerative disease, and a normal life span is possible.
(*Ha'ilono Kina, January 1984, p. 8*)

Toxic Shock Syndrome
This disease is characterized by a high fever, rash, vomiting, diarrhea, muscle weakness, and peeling skin. It is associated with tampon use, as 95 percent of the women affected were found to have been menstruating and using tampons at the time the disease occurred. Although 96 percent of the victims are female, the disease has occurred in men. Some were the husbands of affected women, so it may be that one infects the other. Thirty percent of those who contracted the disease in 1981 died.
(*"Mind and Body,"* Science Digest, *December 1981, p. 102; Cooke and Dworkin, p. 481*)

Track Records, 1983

Distance	World Record: Men	World Record: Women
100 meters	9.93 sec.	10.79 sec.
800 meters	1 min., 41.73 sec.	1 min., 53.28 sec.
5000 meters	13 min., 00.42 sec.	15 min., 8.26 sec.

(*World Almanac, 1984*)

Training of the Sexes
A study of cultures reveals that in most of them, male children are taught to be self-reliant and to achieve.

Girls are taught to be nurturing, responsible, and obedient.

(Hoffman, p. 59)

Tranquilizers
Males: 19 million men have used tranquilizers prescribed by a physician.

Females: 32 million women have utilized tranquilizers prescribed by a physician.

(Levy, p. 196)

Transvestism
(Transvestism is defined as "the impulse to dress in the clothing of the opposite sex.")

Transvestism occurs more frequently among males than among females.

(Kolb, p. 505)

Travel, Air
Male: Seventy-three percent of the air travel that is done for business purposes is done by men. Forty-five percent of the pleasurable air travel is done by men.

Female: Twenty-seven percent of all business-related air travel is done by women. Fifty-five percent of the flights taken for pleasurable purposes are taken by women.

(Reynolds, 11/25/83)

Truck Drivers
97.8 percent of truck drivers are male.

(Hacker, p. 127)

Trunk
A woman's trunk is longer than a man's.

(Dyer, p. 108)

Tune, Carry a
Most females can carry a tune better than males can. (This may be due to their finer auditory memories.)

(Newsweek, 5/18/81, p. 73)

Two Things at Once
As a result of his more specialized brain, a man is able to do two different things at once, such as working on a piece of machinery and carrying on a conversation. Because information is processed in both sides at the same time, rather than in just one side, a woman finds it difficult to do more than one thing at a time.

(Goleman, p. 34)

Typing
Women are better at typing than men, presumably because of their greater fine-motor-coordination skills.

(Newsweek, 5/18/81, p. 73)

Typists
96.9 percent of typists are female.

(Hacker, p. 127)

Ulcers

(An ulcer is a sore that does not heal, either on the skin or in a membrane.)

Male: Ten percent of the male population have an ulcer. Two men for every one woman have an ulcer. (This ratio has dropped sharply since 1960, when ulcers affected ten men for every one woman!)

Female: Five percent of the female population have an ulcer. An ulcer is most likely to develop after menopause when, it is believed, the reduced estrogen supply lessens the woman's protection from infections.

(Man's Body, p. C27)

Undergraduate (College) Students

Males: In 1983, 5.7 million men were enrolled in college.
Females: 5.9 million women were enrolled in college.

(Murphy, p. 50)

Underweight

Females are more likely to be underweight than males are. 23.1 percent of women are underweight, compared to 12 percent of men.

(Geosphere, August 1981, p. 142)

Unemployment

Male: In 1981, 4.4 million men were unemployed.
Female: 5.9 million women were unemployed.

(U.S.A. Statistics in Brief, 1981, p. 145)

Unfaithfulness, Reasons Cited by Opposite Sex
Male: "Because she wants more commitment from her partner than I can give."
Female: "Because he needs sexual variety."
(*Cory, January 1982, p. 24*)

Union Membership
Male: 78.7 percent of all union members are men.
Female: 21.3 percent of union members are women.
(*Bird, p. 119*)

University and College Administrators
36.2 percent of university and college administrators are women.
(*D. Rubin, p. 61*)

University and College Faculty Members
During the academic year ending in June 1981, there were 359,880 full-time faculty members in American colleges and universities. Of these, only 25.5 percent were women. At private colleges and universities, 10 percent of full professors were women and 50.6 percent of the instructors and lecturers were women. At public colleges and universities, women accounted for 9 percent of the full professorships and 51.3 percent of the lecturers and instructors.
(*Hacker, p. 245*)

Upper Body Strength
Men are about 50 percent stronger in the upper body (from the waist up) than women.
(*Wagenvoord/Bailey, Women, p. 95*)

Urethra
Male: The male urethra is twenty centimeters, or eight and a half inches, long.
Female: The female urethra is 3.8 centimeters, or one and a half inches, long.
(*Woman's Body, p. 349*)

Urinary Disorders
Urinary disorders are more common in the female, due to the

close proximity of her urinary system and intestinal tract, which makes bacterial entry into the urinary system easier.

(Woman's Body, p. 63)

Urinary Tract Infections

More women than men suffer urinary tract infections. It is postulated that it may be because the normal secretions of the prostate kill off the bacteria that enter a man's urinary tract.

(Woman's Body, p. 363)

Valium and Breast Enlargement
Male: Some men experience breast enlargement after using Valium.
Female: Breast enlargement is not a reported side effect of Valium use among women.
  (Healthwise, *Vol. 5, No. 1)*

Values, Most Important
Males: Seventy-five percent said the most important part of their lives was their jobs.
Females: Seventy-five percent said the most important aspect of their lives were their families.
  (*Wagenvoord/Bailey,* Women, *p. 272)*

Varicose Veins
Male: One in every four men over forty has varicose veins.
Female: One in every two women over forty suffers from varicose veins. Pregnancy, standing in one spot, distention of the abdomen, and constipation all contribute to this problem.
  (Man's Body, *pp. B28–30)*

Verbal Ability
Females excel at high level verbal tasks, in understanding verbal concepts, in the comprehension of difficult written material, and in fluency in creative writing.
  (*Franks and Burtle, p. 39)*

Veterans
Male: Ninety-eight percent of all war veterans are male.
Female: Two percent of all war veterans are female.
(*Bird, p. 118*)

Veterinary Medicine, Degrees
Male: 67.2 percent of veterinary degrees awarded in the 1979–80 academic year went to men.
Female: 32.8 percent were awarded to women.
(*Hacker, p. 244*)

Veterinary School Students
Male: In 1983, 61 percent of the students at veterinary schools were men.
Female: Thirty-nine percent of the students at veterinary schools were women.
(*Caudle, p. 8*)

Video Games
Girls score just as high as boys on video games after they have had the same amount of practice.
(*Kiesler, Sproull, and Eccles, p. 46*)

Violence and Lovers
Thirty percent of American couples engage in at least one physically violent episode during a relationship.
(*Schuman, p. 69*)

Violent Crimes
Only one in ten violent crimes is committed by a woman.
(*Bird, p. 152*)

Viral Infections
Males are much more prone to viral infections than females are.
(Health, *p. 22*)

Virginity Loss
Males: Forty-three percent of males lose their virginity by the time they are sixteen.

Females: Thirty-one percent of females lose their virginity by the time they are sixteen.

(*Hass,* Parade Magazine, *1/16/83; article by Shearer, p. 12*)

Vision
Male: Men have better daylight vision than women.
Female: Women have better night vision than men.

(*Goleman, p. 59*)

Visits to Physicians
Male: In 1979, 162 million visits to physicians were made by males.
Female: 204 million visits to physicians were made by women in 1979.

(*Census 1980;* Abstract, *p. 107*)

Visual Impairment
Men are more likely to suffer from visual impairment than women are.

(Man's Body, *pp. C05–06*)

Visual-Spatial Ability
Male superiority in visual-spatial tasks becomes evident as early as age six, in contrast to females, whose brain's right hemisphere does not process spatial information as well until they are thirteen or older.

(*Wagenvoord/Bailey,* Women, *p. 25;* Newsweek, *5/18/81, p. 73*)

Vital Capacity
("Vital capacity is the volume of air that is moved through the lungs from a maximum inhalation to a maximum expiration.")

The female's vital capacity is 10 percent less than that of a man of equal size.

(*Klafs and Arnheim, p. 183*)

Vitamin B$_6$
(Vitamin B$_6$ can be found in brewer's yeast, brown rice, beef, leafy green vegetables, bananas, eggs, and milk.)
Male: In a man, vitamin B$_6$ is helpful for sexual disorders such as prostatis (inflammation of the prostate, a male sex gland).

Female: Women have a higher requirement for B$_6$ than men do. It is especially helpful in relieving premenstrual fluid retention.

(Clark, p. 56; Kirschmann, p. 26)

Vitamin E

(Vitamin E is found in cold pressed vegetable oils such as safflower and soybean oil, and in nuts, grains, molasses, and eggs.) *Male:* Vitamin E is helpful for male sexual disorders such as prostatis.
Female: Vitamin E is helpful in regulating scanty or excessive menstrual flow, and for relieving hot flashes and headaches brought on by menopause.

(Kirschmann, p. 53)

Vitamin F

(Vitamin F is found in vegetable oils such as soy or corn. It is also found in cod-liver oil.)

Men need five times the amount of vitamin F women do. It is helpful in sexual disorders such as prostatis. Both sexes need vitamin F for the production of prostaglandins, found in the tissues of the prostate gland, brain, kidney, and seminal and menstrual fluid.

(Kirschmann, p. 57)

Vitamin Purchase and Ingestion

Women purchase three fourths of the vitamins sold. Sixty-one percent of those who take vitamins are female.

(Brothers, p. 18)

Vocational Education

Males: In 1976, 60 percent of the males enrolled in vocational education classes were studying for trades and industrial programs that lead to higher-paying jobs.
Females: 38.7 percent of women in vocational education were studying homemaking skills. Only 4.9 percent were studying for trade and industrial positions that lead to higher-paying jobs.

(Bird, p. 106, from the Department of Health, Education and Welfare)

Voice Changes and Aging

Male: The vocal cords become less flexible as a man ages so he cannot hit the high notes he hit when he was younger.

(Wagenvoord/Bailey, Men, *p. 73)*

Female: A female's voice may become husky at menopause due to the lower supply of estrogen, which results in decreased flexibility of the vocal cords.

(Wagenvoord/Bailey, Women, *p. 76)*

Voice, Pitch

Male: Men have lower voices than women due to the action of testosterone, which causes an increase in the size of the larynx. The outward projection of the larynx is called the Adam's apple.

(Wagenvoord/Bailey, Women, *p. 76)*

Female: Women's voices have a higher pitch than men's, as the vocal cords (the two folds of membranes in the voice box that vibrate to make sounds when air passes over them) are shorter than men's. Women frequently raise the pitch of their voices in ending a sentence. They also speak more softly than men, as they have a range of five tones to a man's three.

(Pine, p. 24)

Voting in the 1980 Election

Male: 59.1 percent of all eligible men voted in the 1980 election.
Female: 59.4 percent of all eligible women voted in the 1980 election.

(Census, 1980)

Voyeurism

More males than females are voyeurs.

(Hyman, p. 642)

Wages: under $10,000 per Year

Women are twice as likely as men to make salaries of less than $10,000 per year.

(Star, 1/24/84, p. 7)

Wages: $10,000–$12,500 per Year

Women who earn yearly salaries of between $10,000 and $12,500 outnumber men two to one.

(Census, 1983; Star, 1/24/84, p. 7)

Wages: $15,000–$30,000 per Year

Men are five times as likely as women to make between $15,000 to $30,000 per year.

(Census, 1982; Star, 1/24/84, p. 7)

Wages: $25,000 and up

Males: In 1983, 12 percent of males earned salaries of $25,000 or more.

Females: 0.8 percent of women earned $25,000 per year or more.

(Kantel, p. 10)

Wages: $50,000 or More per Year

Male: Men are ten times more likely than women to earn $50,000. Two million men earn between $50,000 and $70,000 a year. 1,046,000 men have salaries of greater than $75,000 per year.

Female: 200,000 women earn between $50,000 and $70,000 per year. 114,000 women earn $75,000 or more per year.

(*Census, 1982, Star, 1/24/84, p. 7*)

Wages, Average
Male: In 1983 the average weekly salary for a man was $385.
Female: The average weekly salary for a woman was $252.

(Parade Magazine, *10/30/83, p. 11*)

Wages, College Graduates
Male: In 1981 the average yearly pay for men in the United States was $19,433.
Female: In 1981 the average yearly pay for women in the United States was $12,028. (For every $100 earned by a man, a woman earned $59.)

(*Kantel, p. 10*)

Wages, Lifetime
Male: Male high school graduates can expect to earn $861,000 in their lifetimes. Male college graduates can expect to earn $1,190,000 in their lifetimes.
Female: Female high school graduates can expect to earn $381,000 in their lifetimes. Female college graduates can expect to earn $861,000 in their lifetimes.

(*Shearer, p. 8*)

Wages, Median for Full-time Workers
Male: The Median wage for full-time male workers is $20,172.
Female: The Median wage for full-time female workers is $12,172.

(*Oman, p. 175*)

Wages, 1983
In 1983, a woman earned 62 cents for every dollar earned by a man (this was two cents more than she earned in 1939). Women with college degrees earned less than men with eighth-grade educations.

(*D. Rubin, p. 59; Kantel, p. 10*)

Wages, Professional
Male: The 1983 census indicated that the median income for professional men was $23,126.
Female: The median income for professional women was $15,285.
(Hacker, p. 148)

Wages, Weekly
Women make 66 percent of what a man earns weekly. Professional women make 71 percent of what professional men earn on a weekly basis.
(D. Rubin, p. 59)

Wages by Profession
ACCOUNTANTS:
Male: In 1983 male accountants earned an average $468 per week.
Female: Female accountants earned an average $325 per week.
(D. Rubin, p. 61)
ARMED FORCES:
Women earn as much money as men do in the armed forces.
(Kantel, p. 11)
ATTORNEYS:
Male: In 1982 the average income of a male attorney was $653 per week.
Female: The average income for a female attorney was $492 per week.
(D. Rubin, p. 61)
BANK OFFICIALS:
Male: The average wage for male bank officials is $571 per week.
Female: The average wage for female bank officials is $336 per week.
(D. Rubin, p. 61)
BARTENDERS:
In 1981, for every $1,000 earned by a male bartender, a female bartender earned $844.
(Hacker, p. 122)
BLUE-COLLAR SUPERVISORS
In 1981, for every $1,000 earned by a male blue-collar supervisor, a female earned $642.
(Hacker, p. 122)

BOOKKEEPERS:

In 1982, female bookkeepers earned an average of $98 less per week than male bookkeepers earned. (Women held 90.6 percent of the bookkeeping jobs.)

   (Porter, p. 22)

BUYER, WHOLESALE AND RETAIL:

Male: A male buyer earns an average of $412 per week.

Female: A female buyer earns an average of $271 per week.

   (D. Rubin, p. 61)

CASHIERS:

In 1981, for every $1,000 earned by a male cashier, a female made $920.

   (Hacker, p. 122)

CHEMIST:

Male: A male chemist, recently graduated from college, earns an average of $19,600 per year.

Female: A female chemist, recently graduated from college, earns an average of $19,000 per year.

   (D. Rubin, p. 61)

CLERICAL WORKERS:

Male: The median salary of a male clerical worker is $18,671.

Female: The median salary of a female clerical worker is $10,997.

   (Hacker, p. 148)

COLLEGE TEACHERS:

In 1981, female college teachers were earning $803 for every $1,000 earned by male college teachers.

   (Hacker, p. 122)

COMPUTER OPERATORS:

Male: $18,849 is the average starting salary for male computer operators.

Female: $15,135 is the average starting salary for female computer operators.

   (Kantel, p. 12)

COMPUTER PROGRAMMERS:

In 1981, a female computer programmer earned $736 for every $1,000 earned by a male computer programmer.

   (Hacker, p. 122)

COMPUTER SPECIALIST:

Males: In 1982, male computer specialists earned an average of $546 per week.

Females: Female computer specialists earned an average of $420 per week.

(Porter, p. 22)

COMPUTER SYSTEMS ANALYSTS:

In 1982 female computer systems analysts earned an average of $420 per week, while their male counterparts earned $546.

(Porter, p. 22)

COOKS:

In 1981, for every $1,000 earned by a male cook, a female cook earned $734.

(Hacker, p. 122)

DESIGNERS:

Male: In 1983 male designers made an average of $526 per week.
Female: Female designers made an average of $302 per week.

(D. Rubin, p. 61)

EDITORS:

Males: In 1982 the average weekly wage of editors was $382.
Females: The average weekly wage for female editors was $324.

(Time, 7/12/82, p. 23)

ELEMENTARY AND SECONDARY SCHOOL ADMINISTRATORS:

In 1979, male elementary and secondary school administrators earned an average of $520 per week, and their female counterparts earned an average of $363 per week.

(Porter, p. 22)

ELEMENTARY SCHOOL TEACHERS:

Although women held 82.2 percent of the elementary school teaching jobs in 1979, they earned an average of $68 less per week than their male counterparts.

(Porter, p. 22)

ENGINEERS:

Male: In 1983 the average weekly wage of a male engineer was $592.
Female: The average weekly wage of a female engineer was $479.

(D. Rubin, p. 61)

HEADS OF HOUSEHOLDS:

In 1982 female heads of households earned only 47 percent of what male heads of households earned.

(Porter, p. 22)

HEALTH ADMINISTRATORS:

In 1980, female health administrators earned $655 for every $1,000 earned by a male health administrator.

(Hacker, p. 122)

HEALTH TECHNICIANS:

In 1982 male health technicians earned an average weekly wage of $324 while women earned only $273 per week.

(Porter, p. 22)

INSURANCE AGENTS:

In 1980, for every $1,000 earned by a male insurance agent, a female insurance agent earned only $643.

(Hacker, p. 122)

LAWYERS:

In 1981, female lawyers earned $710 for every $1,000 earned by male lawyers.

(Hacker, p. 122)

MANAGERS:

Male: In 1980 the median salary of male managers was $23,558.
Female: The median salary of female managers was $12,936.

(Hacker, p. 148)

MANAGERS AND ADMINISTRATORS:

Male: In 1982 the average yearly wage for a manager or administrator was $23,558.
Female: The average wage for a female manager or administrator was $12,936 per year.

(Porter, p. 22)

NURSES:

Male: In 1982 male nurses made an average of $344 per week.
Female: Female nurses made an average of $326 per week.

(Time, 7/12/82, p. 23)

NURSING AIDES AND ORDERLIES:

In 1980, for every $1,000 earned by a male nursing aide or orderly, a female earned only $822.

(Hacker, p. 122)

OFFICE-MACHINE OPERATORS:

In 1980, a female office-machine operator earned $688 for every $1,000 earned by a male office-machine operator.

(Hacker, p. 122)

OFFICE MANAGERS:
In 1981, female office managers earned $655 for every $1,000 earned by male office managers.
(*Hacker, p. 122*)

PACKERS AND WRAPPERS:
In 1980, for every $1,000 earned by a male packer and wrapper, a female of the same vocation made $854.
(*Hacker, p. 122*)

PERSONNEL WORKERS:
In 1980, for every $1,000 earned by a male personnel manager, a female personnel manager earned only $643.
(*Hacker, p. 122*)

PHYSICIANS:
Males: In 1983 the average yearly income for male physicians was $70,000.
Females: The average yearly income for female physicians was $45,000.
(*Kantel, p. 12*)

PHYSICIANS AND DENTISTS:
In 1980, for every $1,000 made by a male dentist or physician, a female dentist or physician made $809.
(*Hacker, p. 122*)

POSTAL CLERKS:
In 1980, for every $1,000 made by a male postal clerk, a female made $939.
(*Hacker, p. 122*)

PUBLIC RELATIONS SPECIALISTS:
Males: In 1983, men in public relations averaged annual salaries of $26,803.
Females: Women in public relations averaged salaries of about $18,733 per year.
(*Kantel, p. 12*)

REAL ESTATE AGENTS:
In 1980, female real estate agents earned $709 for every $1,000 male real estate agents earned.
(*Hacker, p. 181*)

REPORTERS:
Male: Male reporters earn an average of $382 per week.
Female: Female reporters earn an average of $324 per week.
(*Time, 7/12/82, p. 23*)

SALES:

Male: In 1980 the median annual salary of male sales workers was $19,910.

Female: The median annual salary for female sales workers was $9,748.

(*Hacker, p. 148*)

Male: In 1982 the average weekly salary for male salespersons was $366.

Female: Female salespersons earned an average of $190 per week.

(Time, 7/12/82, p. 23)

SCHOOL ADMINISTRATORS:

In 1980–1981, female school administrators earned $699 for every $1,000 earned by a male school administrator.

(*Hacker, p. 122*)

SECURITY GUARDS:

In 1981, for every $1,000 made by a male security guard, a woman security guard made $907.

(*Hacker, p. 122*)

SERVICE WORKERS, NONMILITARY:

Male: In 1982 the average nonmilitary male worker in the services earned $238 per week.

Female: The average female service worker earned $170 per week.

(Time, 7/12/82, p. 23)

SOCIAL SCIENTISTS:

In 1981, a female social scientist earned $749 for every $1,000 earned by a male social scientist.

(*Hacker, p. 122*)

Male: A male social scientist earns an average of $580 per week.

Female: A female social scientist earns an average of $420 per week.

(*D. Rubin, p. 61*)

TEACHERS, ELEMENTARY:

Male: In 1981, male elementary school teachers made an average of $379 per week.

Female: Female elementary teachers made an average of $311 per week.

(Time, 7/12/82, p. 23)

TEACHERS, HIGH SCHOOL:
In 1981, for every $1,000 made by a male high school teacher, a female high school teacher made $829.
(*Hacker, p. 122*)

UNIVERSITY TEACHERS:
Male: Male university teachers earn an average of $528 per week.
Female: Female university teachers earn an average of $415 per week.
(*D. Rubin, p. 61*)

VOCATIONAL OR EDUCATIONAL COUNSELORS:
Male: A male vocational or educational counselor earns an average of $459 per week.
Female: A female vocational or educational counselor earns an average of $348 per week.
(*D. Rubin, p. 61*)

Wakefulness
Male infants are awake for longer periods than female infants are.
(*Newsweek, 5/18/81, p. 73*)

Waking Up
Women are more easily awakened than men, and most women (of any age) will awaken to a baby's cry. Men are harder to arouse and will awaken to a baby's cry only if they have been a father.
(*Researcher: William Wilson, M.D.; Duke University, and William Zung, M.D., in* Science Digest, *January 1982, p. 101*)

Walking
Because a woman's hips are wider than a man's, she will tend to sway her hips in order to move forward.
(*Brothers, Woman's Day, 2/9/82, p. 138*)

Warmth
Women feel warmer in winter due to the extra fat under their skin.
(*Brothers, Woman's Day, 2/9/82, p. 138*)

Water
Male: The male body is made up of from 60 percent to 70 percent water.
Female: The female body is made up of about 50 percent to 60 percent water.
(Woman's Body, *p. 273;* Good Looks, *p. 20*)

Wechsler Adult Intelligence Scale
Male: Men excel on the Wechsler IQ test in numerical reasoning, mechanical aptitude, and gross motor skills.
Female: Women excel in the areas of memory, detail, and verbal ability.
(*The Diagram Group, p. 299*)

Weight and Height
Male: The average male is five feet nine inches tall and weighs 155 pounds.
Female: The average female is five feet three inches tall and weighs 125 pounds.
(*Wagenvoord/Bailey,* Men, *p. 203*)

Weight at Birth
Male: Boys weigh an average of seven and four-fifths pounds at birth.
Female: Girls weigh an average of seven and two-fifths pounds at birth.
(Woman's Body, *pp. A05–06*)

Weight Loss
Male: It is easier for men to lose weight than it is for women, and the rate of their weight loss is usually steadier and more predictable. A man's metabolism is higher than a woman's, and, since he is more muscular, he needs five more calories per pound per day to maintain himself.
Female: Weight loss is harder for women than men. In women, the rate of weight loss tends to be erratic due to the difference in her body fat composition, her tendency to retain water as a result of the activity of the hormone estrogen, and her lower metabolism. Most women need about ten calories per pound per day to maintain themselves.
(*Edelstein, pp. 11–15*)

The average dieter loses sixteen pounds when dieting. Men lose a little more than women do.

(*Ubell, p. 13*)

Weight of Primary Organs

The male brain is heavier than the female brain. The male heart is heavier than the female heart.

(Man's Body, pp. A22–24)

Weight Ranges

Male: For every one hundred men, ninety-five weigh between 127 and 209.

Female: For every one hundred women, ninety-five weigh between 95 and 195.

(Man's Body, pp. A19–21)

Weight Training

Women can train as hard as men but will not develop massive muscles as they lack the high levels of muscle-building testosterone that men have. Men are stronger, so they can lift heavier weights, but women can hold weights longer than men can.

(*Reynolds, p. 8*)

Welders

94.7 percent of welders are male.

(*Hacker, p. 128*)

Wet Dreams

Male: Almost all men have experienced orgasm while dreaming.

Female: Many studies indicate that over half of the females interviewed had experienced orgasm while dreaming. One study indicated that two thirds of them had.

(*Wagenvoord/Bailey*, Women, *p. 125*)

Whooping Cough

Males are more likely than females to suffer from whooping cough (as with many other respiratory diseases).

(Man's Body, pp. C01–04)

Widows and Widowers, Living Alone
Widows and widowers are currently the largest group of Americans who live alone, numbering about 7.7 million. Widows outnumber widowers by six to one.
(Sanoff, p. 56)

Widows and Widowers, Mortality of
Widowers: Death occurs two times as often among the widowed as among the married. Suicide is the third ranking cause of death among widowers.
Widows: The cancer rate of widows is six times that of married women in the same age range, but widows do not die as early as widowers.
(Modern Maturity, *12/81-1/82, p. 12*)

Work, and Enjoyment
Women are as satisfied with their jobs as men are.
(Psychology Today Survey on Work, *Renwick and Lawler, the* Psychology Today *Staff, p. 53*)

Work, and Its Importance According to Sex
In several studies, it has been shown that the career of the man still comes first when it comes to making a move to another town. Apparently, the man's job is still considered by both sexes to be more important than the woman's, regardless of salary.
(Renwick, Lawler, and the Psychology Today *Staff, Survey on Work, p. 62)*

Work, and Sense of Worth
Work is just as crucial to a man's sense of worth as to a woman's.
(Time, *7/12/82, p. 23*)

Work, Motivation Among Middle Management
Both male and female managers want high pay and promotions as their rewards for good work. (Studies often indicate that women are not motivated to work for money. This study refutes that idea.)
(Human Behavior, *March 1977, p. 49*)

Work, Reasons for
Male: Men say they are working for their family, for personal satisfaction, and for economic reasons.

Female: Women say they are working for personal satisfaction, and for economic reasons.

   (*Porter, p. 22*)

Workaholics
(Those who work fifty or more hours per week)

   Female workaholics have higher divorce rates than male workaholics. Thirty-five percent of female workaholics never marry, whereas only 9 percent of workaholic men never marry.

   (*Elias, p. 1*)

Work Days Lost Due to Illness
Male: In 1979 men missed an average of 4.7 work days due to illness.

Female: Women lost an average of 5.4 days due to illness.

   (*Census, p.118*)

Work Force over Age 20
Male: Seventy-five percent of men over the age of twenty are working.

Female: Fifty-one percent of women over the age of twenty are in the work force.

   (*Hershey, p. 1*)

Work Hours of the Day
Male: Men average 6.3 hours a day at work and 1.6 hours with the family.

Female: Working women spend an average of 5.3 hours a day at work and spend about 4.8 hours with the family.

   (*Lingeman, p. 10*)

Working Even If Rich
Male: In a survey of 7,281 adults conducted by the University of Kentucky, 74 percent of the males interviewed said they would work even if rich. Seventy-two percent to 73.8 percent of the married men interviewed said they would work if rich.

Female: 64.4 percent of the women interviewed said they would quit their jobs if they had "enough money to live comfortably." In the same survey, 60.2 percent of the married women interviewed said they would quit their jobs if rich.

   (*Zimmerman, front page*)

Working Harder

Male: Men take an average of fifty-two minutes off from work in scheduled or unscheduled breaks.

Female: Women take fewer breaks and expend more energy on the job than men. Women take a total of thirty-five minutes in breaks a day and put out 112 percent of the effort that men do on their jobs. (Unmarried women work the hardest on the job and take the fewest breaks.)

    (Fogg, p. 18)

Worklife Expectancy

Male: The average working man has a worklife expectancy of forty-three years.

Female: The average working married woman has a worklife expectancy of twenty-five years; the single woman has a worklife expectancy of forty-five years.

    (Porter, p. 22)

Writers, Erotic

Women of today are writing as sexually explicitly as men are.

    (Cary, pp. 47–49)

Z

Zinc, Need for
(Zinc is found in meat products, eggs, wheat germ, and brewer's yeast.)

Male: Low levels of zinc can result in lowered sperm counts in men.

Female: Zinc can be helpful in regulating irregular menstrual periods.

(Mindell, p. 120)

Bibliography

"AAUW Is Strong Advocate in Congress for Women in Math, Science and Technology." *Graduate Woman*, September 1983, Vol. 377, No. 5.

About Schizophrenia. South Deerfield, Mass.: Channing L. Bete Co., 1981.

Adams, Virginia. "Getting at the Heart of Jealous Love." *Psychology Today*, May 1980, p. 38.

Adams, Virginia. "Jane Crow in the Army." *Psychology Today*, October 1980, p. 50.

"Aging." *Human Behavior*, July 1978.

Anderson, Duncan. "Machines." *Science Digest*, April 1982, p. 96.

Anderson, Richard. Reported by Jay Branegan and Anne Constable. "What Are Prisons For?" *Time*, 9/13/82, p. 38.

Angier, Natalie. "Marijuana: Bad News and Good." *Annual Editions of Health*, 83/84. Guildford, Conn.: Dushken Publishing Co., 1983.

Angier, Natalie. "The Case Against Steroids." *Discover*, November 1983, p. 98.

Arkoff, Abe. *Psychology and Personal Growth.* New York: Allyn and Bacon, 1975.

Atchley, Robert, and Mildred Seltzer. *The Sociology of Aging: Selected Readings.* Belmont, Calif.: Wadsworth Publishing Company, 1976.

Avery, Patricia. "With ERA Dying, What's Ahead for Women's Groups?" *U.S. News & World Report*, 6/28/82, p. 55.

Barrett, Katherine. "AIDS: What It Does to a Family." *Ladies' Home Journal*, November 1983, p. 98.

"Beating Up Hubby." *Human Behavior*, November 1978 (from research by Murray Straus, Suzanne Steinmetz, and Richard Gelles, University of New Hampshire), p. 80.

"Beauty and the Mating Game." *Ms.*, December 1983, p. 8.

Behrman, Richard E., and Victor C. Vaughn, III, eds. *Nelson Textbook of Pediatrics*. Philadelphia: W. B. Saunders and Co., 1983, pp. 1837, 1846, 1849.

Bellinger, David C., and Jean Berko Gleason. "Sex Differences in Directives to Young Children." *Sex Roles: A Journal of Research*, Vol. 8, No. 11, November 1982, p. 1123.

Bennet, William. "Medical Forum." *The Harvard Medical School Healthletter*, Vol. 5, No. 1, November 1979, p. 2.

Bernard, Jesse. *The Future of Marriage*. New York: Bantam World Publishing Company, 1972.

Billies, Laurie, Ph.D. "Getting Strong." *Shape*, November 1981, p. 83.

"Binge-Purge Syndrome." "Lifestyle," *Newsweek*, 11/2/81, p. 60.

Bird, Caroline. *What Women Want* (Statement by Commissioners, Delegates, and Observers at the National Women's Conference), Houston, Texas, November 1977.

Bishop, Jerry. "Gene Defect May Solve Mysteries." *Wall Street Journal*, 1/29/82, p. 1.

"The Body: When Women Rape Men." *Omni*, December 1982, p. 28.

Boyd, Lou. *Honolulu Advertiser*, 7/1/82, p. 24.

Boyd, Lou. "Just Checking," *Honolulu Advertiser*, 11/18/83, p. A26.

Boyd, Lou. "Just Checking," *Honolulu Advertiser*, 12/15/83, p. E18.

"Boys' Math Scores." "Global Report," *Honolulu Advertiser*, 11/28/83, pp. D4–12.

"Breaking Through: Women on the Move." *U.S. News & World Report*, 11/20/82, p. 50.

"Breakthroughs." *Health*, May 1982, pp. 22, 23.

Brenner, Charles. *An Elementary Textbook of Psychoanalysis*. Garden City, New York: Doubleday, 1955.

"Bride and Grooming." *Human Behavior*, April 1977, p. 37.

Bridgewater, Carol. "Dedicated Female Managers." *Psychology Today*, February 1984, p. 17.

Brody, Jane. "Distinct Health Advantages Found in Vegetarian Diets." *Honolulu Star Bulletin*, 2/3/84, p. A16.

Brothers, Joyce. "Men and Women: The Differences." *Woman's Day*, 2/9/82, p. 58.

Brothers, Joyce. *What Every Woman Should Know About Men.* New York: Simon & Schuster, 1981.

Brucklen, Mark. "Things Here and There." *Prevention*, January 1980, p. 77.

Buchsbaum, Monte S. "The Sensoristat in the Brain." *Psychology Today*, May 1978, p. 96.

Candance, Lyle Hogan. "Women in Sports." *Cosmopolitan*, September 1980, p. 269.

Cary, Meredith. "Sexual Writers." *Human Behavior*, December 1977, p. 47.

Caudle, Sheila. "Status of Women in Education." *Honolulu Advertiser*, 8/28/83.

"Cellulite: Hard to Budge Pudge." *Consumer*, Department of Health, Education and Human Services Publication No. 80-1078.

Chestnutt, Jane. "New Light on What Causes Obesity." *Woman's Day*, 10/5/82, p. 56.

Child Abuse and Neglect. The Problem and Its Management. U.S. Department of Health, Education and Welfare. Office of Human Development/Office of Child Development, Children's Bureau, National Center on Child Abuse and Neglect, Vol. 2 (undated).

Clark, Linda. *The Best of Linda Clark.* New Canaan, Connecticut: Keats Publishing Company, 1976.

Clarke, Gary. "Taking a Look at the Women We Watch on T.V." *Woman's Day*, 10/5/82.

Cocks, Jay. "How Long Till Equality?" *Time*, 7/12/82, p. 20.

Collier, James. "It Is Different for Women." *Reader's Digest*, January 1983, p. 84.

Columbu, Franco. *Franco Columbu's Complete Book of Body Training.* Chicago: Contemporary Books, 1982.

Cooke, Cynthia, M.D., and Susan Dworkin. *The Ms. Guide to a Woman's Health.* New York: Berkley, 1979.

Cooley, Donald. *After 40 Medical and Health Guide.* Better Homes and Gardens Books. Des Moines: Meredith Corporation, 1980.

"Coping with Jealousy." "Social Behavior," *Human Behavior*, March 1977, p. 30.

Corliss, Richard. Reported by Martha Smilgis, Denis Worrel. "The New Ideal of Beauty." *Time*, 8/30/82.

Cory, Christopher. "Newsline," *Psychology Today*, October 1978, p. 44.

Cory, Christopher. "Newsline," *Psychology Today*, April 1980.

Cory, Christopher. "Newsline," *Psychology Today*, October 1980.

Cory, Christopher. "Newsline," *Psychology Today*, January 1981.

Cory, Christopher. "Newsline," *Psychology Today*, November 1981, p. 20.

Cory, Christopher. "Newsline," *Psychology Today*, December 1981, p. 19.

Cory, Christopher. "What Makes a Partner Unfaithful?" *Psychology Today*, January 1982, p. 24.

Cory, Christopher. "Newsline," *Psychology Today*, April 1982, p. 20.

Crockett, Art. *Stay Young Forever*. Miami: Merit, 1980.

"Crosstalk," *Psychology Today*, January 1983, pp. 14, 56.

"Crosstalk," *Psychology Today*, February 1983, pp. 16. 72.

Davidson, Lynne, and Duberman, Lucile. "Friendship: Common Interactional Patterns in Same Sex Dyads." *Sex Roles: A Journal of Research*, Vol. 8, No. 8, August 1982.

Davis, Flora. "How Much Drinking Is Too Much?" *Woman's Day*, 7/8/80.

Davis, Flora. "How to Read Men." *Woman's Day*, 11/15/83, p. 98.

DeRosis, Helen, M.D., and Victoria Pellegrino. *The Book of Hope: How Women Overcome Depression*. New York: Macmillan, 1976.

The Diagram Group. *The Brain: A User's Manual*. New York: Berkley Books, 1983, p. 259.

————. *Man's Body*. New York: Bantam, 1978.

Dowd, Maureen. "Rape: The Sexual Weapon." *Time*, 9/5/83, p. 27.

Dowling, Collette. *The Cinderella Complex*. New York: Pocket Books, 1981.

Dranov, Paula. "Why Women Live Longer." *Science Digest*, May 1981, p. 32.

"Drugs in Study Reduce Blood Clotting." *Honolulu Advertiser*, 11/18/83, p. A29.

Duff, Susan. "Your Medical Beauty Shape-Up for Legs." *Self,* May 1980, p. 84.

Durden-Smith, Jo, and Diane DeSimone. "Hidden Threads of Illness." *Science Digest,* January 1984, p. 53.

Dustan, Harriet, M.D. *What Every Woman Should Know about Depression.* South Deerfield, Mass.: Channing L. Bete Co., 1980.

Dyer, K. F., with Bob Wischnia. "Why Men Run Faster than Women." *Runner's World,* November 1983, p. 64.

Eastman, Peggy. "Hormones: Chemical Busybodies." *Self,* September 1981, p. 94.

Edelson, Edward. "Woman's Day Medifacts." *Woman's Day,* 1/11/83, p. 23.

Edelstein, Barbara. *The Woman's Doctor's Diet for Women.* New York: Ballantine Books, 1977.

Ehrenreich, Barbara, and Karin Stallard. "The Nouveau Poor." *Ms,* July/August 1982, p. 219.

Eiseman, Ben, M.D. "What Are My Chances?" *Family Circle,* 5/19/81, p. 48.

Elias, Marilyn. "Women Pay for Working Hard." "Life," *U.S.A. Today,* 2/7/84, p. 1.

Engles, George. "Emotional Stress and Sudden Death." *Psychology Today,* November 1977, pp. 114–153.

Eppingham, John. "How Different Are Men and Women?" *National Enquirer,* 11/24/81, p. 37.

Espner, Will. *How to Increase Your Lifespan.* Hilldale, Calif.: S S and B Publishing Co., 1978.

"Facts: Scleroderma." *Ha'ilono Kina,* Commission on the Handicapped, December 1983, Vol. 49.

"The Family." *Human Behavior,* February 1977, p. 35.

Family Circle, September 1975, p. 130.

Farnham-Diggory, Sylvia. *Learning Disabilities.* Cambridge: Harvard University Press, 1978.

"Feminine Fantasies in Feminism." *Human Behavior,* November 1978, p. 50.

"Fiddle, Faddle, Fun and Fury." *New Woman,* November-December 1979, p. 10.

"Fiddle, Faddle, Fun and Fury." *New Woman,* July-August 1980, p. 12.

"Fiddle, Faddle, Fun and Fury." *New Woman,* September-October, 1980, p. 14.

Field, Anne. "The Powers That Be." *Ms.,* December 1982, p. 78.

Finkelhor, David. *Sexually Victimized Children.* Free Press, 1979. Reviewed in *In Response to Violence in the Family,* Vol. 1, July 1980, p. 7.

Firth, Michael. "Sex Discrimination in Job Opportunities for Women." *Sex Roles: A Journal of Research,* Vol. 8, No. 8, August 1982.

Flowers, Charles, Jr., M.D., and Maxine Abrams. "Sexuality: A Guide to Total Understanding." *Cosmopolitan,* March 1980, p. 227.

Fogg, Susan. "Working Harder." University of Michigan study, *Honolulu Star Bulletin,* January 17, 1980, p. 17.

Foley, Denise. "Why Do Women Live Longer?" *Prevention,* April 1984, pp. 56–61.

Ford, Edward. *Why Marriage?* Niles, Illinois: Argus Communications, 1974.

Foreman, Judy. *Honolulu Star Bulletin,* 12/12/81, p. C1.

Frank, Ellen, Ph.D., and Sondra Forsyth Enos. "The Lovelife of the American Wife."

Frankfort, Ellen. *Vaginal Politics.* New York: Bantam Books, 1972.

Franks, Violet, and Vasanti Burtle, eds. *Women in Therapy: New Psychotherapies for a Changing World.* New York: Brunner/Mazel, Inc., 1974.

Friermuth, Donna. "Personal File," *Human Behavior,* July 1977, p. 44; May 1970, p. 13.

Fromer, Margot. "Motion Sickness: All in Your Head." *Psychology Today,* January 1983.

Fryer, Douglas, Edwin Henry, and Charles Sparks. *General Psychology,* p. 242. New York: Barnes and Noble, Inc., 1954.

Gardner, A. Ward, M.D. *Good Housekeeping Dictionary of Symptoms.* New York: Ace Books, Grosset & Dunlap, 1982.

Gelman, David, et al. "Just How the Sexes Differ." *Newsweek,* 5/18/81.

Gelman, Eric. "In Sports: Lions vs. Tigers." *Newsweek,* 5/18/81, p. 75.

Georgakas, Dan. *The Methuselah Factors.* New York: Simon & Schuster, 1980.

Geosphere, August 1981, p. 142.

Gilligan, Carol. "Why Should a Woman Be More Like a Man?" *Psychology Today,* June 1982, p. 68.

Gilmartin, Brian. "That Swinging Couple Down the Block." *Psychology Today,* February 1975, p. 55.

Girdano, Daniel, and George Everly. *Controlling Stress and Tension.* Englewood Cliffs, N.J.: Prentice Hall, 1979.

Gittleson, Bernard. *Biorhythms: A Perfect Science.* New York: Warner Books, Arco Publishing Company, 1978.

Glassman, Carl. "Sunny Side Up; Rainy Day Blues." *Ladies' Home Journal,* November 1980, p. 74.

Goleman, Daniel. "Special Abilities of the Sexes. Do They Begin in the Brain?" *Psychology Today,* November 1978, p. 48.

Good Looks, December 1981, p. 20.

Gottlieb, Annie. "Men and Women: What Differences Do the Differences Really Make?" *Mademoiselle,* July 1981.

Gould, Roger, M.D. "How to Be Strong and Secure." *Woman's Day,* 5/19/78, p. 54.

Grant, Alexander, M.D., editor. *Healthwise,* sample issue, 1982.

Grant, Alexander. *Healthwise,* Vol. 5, No. 2, p. 1.

"The Great American Smokeout, 1983." *Honolulu Advertiser,* 11/18/83, p. A29.

"Great Preview: The 1980 Census." *Working Woman,* September 1980.

Greenberger, Robert. "Burning Issue: Woman Firefighters Still Spark Resentment in Strongly Macho Job." *Wall Street Journal,* 2/3/83, p. 1.

Griffin, John. "Technosexism." *Honolulu Advertiser,* 12/11/83, p. 2.

Grollman, Arthur. *Clinical Physiology: The Functional Pathology of Disease.* New York: McGraw-Hill, 1957.

Gross, Leonard. "How Men Grow Up Sexually." *Glamour,* December 1980, p. 206.

Guilford, J. P. "Factors Related to Creative Thinking." *Readings in General Psychology.* Edited by Lester Crow and Alice Crow. New York: Barnes and Noble, 1955.

Hacker, Andrew. *U.S.: A Statistical Portrait of the American People.* New York: Viking Press, 1983. Penguin Books.

Hagen, Richard. *The Biosexual Factor.* Garden City, New York: Doubleday, 1979.

Ha'ilono Kina, November 1981, Vol. 24.

Ha'ilono Kina, Commission on the Handicapped, Department of Health, State of Hawaii. November 1983, Vol. 48. January 1984, Vol. 50.

Hammar, Sherral, M.D. "Adolescence." Reprint. *Brenneman's*

Practice of Pediatrics, Chapter 6. Hagerstown, Md.: Harper & Row, 1970.

Hammer, Signe. "The Sexes." *Health*, July 1983, pp. 18–31.

Harmon, Judith, M.D. "Study on Incest." *The Harvard Medical School Healthletter*, Vol. VI, No. 5.

Hartson, Merrill. "His and Hers Survey Confirms a Disparity." *Honolulu Star Bulletin*, 11/2/83, p. A30.

Harvard Medical School Healthletter, March 1981, Vol. VI, No. 5.

Hassett, James, and John Houlihan. "Different Jokes for Different Folks." *Psychology Today*, January 1979, p. 64.

Health, January 1982, Vol. 14, No. 1.

Health and Longevity Report, 11/15/83, Vol. 2, No. 3, p. 1.

Healthwise, Vol. 5.

Heiman, Julia. "Women's Sexual Arousal." *Psychology Today*, April 1975, p. 91.

Hellman, Hal. "Guiding Light." *Psychology Today*, April 1982, p. 22.

Hershey, Robert D. "Rate of Jobless Declined in May to 7.4% in Nation." *New York Times*, June 2, 1984, p. 1.

Hoffman, Joyce. "Alcohol and Sex." *Prevention*, October 1981, p. 68.

Hoffman, Lois. "Changes in Family Roles, Socialization and Sex Differences." *Family Factbook*. Dr. Helena Znaniecki LoPata, Consulting Editor. Chicago: Marquis Academic Media, 1978, p. 59.

Horn, Patrice. "Newsline," *Psychology Today*, December 1976.

Horn, Jack. "Newsline," *Psychology Today*, January 1977, p. 20.

Horn, Jack. "Newsline," *Psychology Today*, October 1977, pp. 45–46.

Horn, Jack. "Newsline," *Psychology Today*, February 1978, pp. 26–37.

Horn, Jack. "Newsline," *Psychology Today*, September 1978, p. 27.

Horn, Jack. "Campus Watch," *Psychology Today*, September 1979, p. 77.

Horn, Jack. "Newsline," *Psychology Today*, November 1980. p. 28.

Horn, Jack. "Newsline," *Psychology Today*, April 1982, p. 20.

"How Long Till Equality?" *Time*, 7/12/82, p. 20.

"How Sex Makes You Healthier." *Everywoman*, November 1981, p. 58.

Hubbard, Ruth, and Marian Lowe. *Genes and Gender*. New York: Guardian Press, 1979.

Hughes, Michael, and Walter Gove. "Playing Dumb." *Psychology Today*, October 1977, p. 72.

Human Behavior. "Behind College Aspirations," February 1977, p. 35.

————. "Female Felons," November 1978, p. 12.

————. "Tools for a Woman's Trade," October 1977, p. 72.

————. "Women Mean Business," March 1977, p. 49.

Hunt, Morton. "The Sexes." Psychology Today, January 1984, p. 17.

Hyman, Harold. The Complete Home Medical Encyclopedia. New York: Avon, 1973.

In Response to Violence in the Family. Vol. 4, No. 6, July/August, 1981, p. 1.

Information Please Almanac 1983. New York: Simon & Schuster, 1982.

"Intelligence." *Parade*, 2/2/82.

James, Barbara. "Answers to Questions," *Medical Aspects of Human Sexuality*, Vol. 17, No. 6, June 1983.

Jencks, Christopher. "Divorced Mothers, Unite!" *Psychology Today*, November 1982, p. 73.

Jones, Ben, and Oscar A. Parsons. "Alcohol and Consciousness Getting High and Coming Down." *Psychology Today*, January 1975, p. 53.

Jones, Jack. "Attractive Men Really Do Have More Fun—A Study Says So." *Honolulu Star Bulletin*, 4/14/82, p. C1.

Kako'o. "Alzheimer's Disease and Related Disorders." Honolulu Chapter (undated, unnumbered).

Kantel, Thelma. "What Women Earn." *Parade*, 9/6/81, p. 10.

Kantel, Thelma. *Parade* in *Honolulu Advertiser*, 7/10/83, p. 5.

Kart, Cary, and Barbara Manard. *Aging in America*. Port Washington, N.Y.: Alfred Publishing Co., 1976.

Kaufman, David, M.D. "The Fundamentals of Fat." *The Physical Educator*, Vol. 32, No. 2, May 1972, p. 77.

Keeley, Jane. "Speaker for the House." *Good Housekeeping*, February 1984, p. 25.

Kiesler, Sara, Lee Sproull, and Jacquelynne S. Eccles. "Second Class Citizens." *Psychology Today*, March 1983.

Kilgore, James. "You May Be Able to Avoid Breaking Up." *New Woman*, January-February 1980, pp. 76–77.

Kirk, Stuart, and Aaron Rosenblatt. "Social Roles of Women in Medicine, Psychiatry, and Social Work." *American Journal of Orthopsychiatry*, Vol. 52, No. 3, July 1982, p. 430.

Kirschmann, John. *Nutrition Almanac*. New York: McGraw-Hill, 1975.

Kissebah, Ahmed. "The Lowdown on Lower Body Fat." *Health*, May 1982.

Klafs, Carl, and Daniel Arnheim. *Modern Principles of Athletic Training*. New York: C. V. Mosby Co., 1981; 5th Edition.

Kleinke. Chris, Richard Staneski, and Jeanne Mason. "Sex Differences in Coping with Depression." *Sex Roles: A Journal of Research*. New York: Plenum Press, Vol. 8, No. 8, August 1982.

Knee Owner's Manual. Patient Information Library. Daly City, Calif.: Krames Communication, 1983.

Knickerbocker, Laura, and Alan J. Bankman. "Anorexia Nervosa—More Than Just a Teenager's Disease." *Cosmopolitan*, August 1981, p. 130.

Kolata, Gina. "Equal Time for Women." *Discover*, January 1984, p. 24.

Kolb, L. *Modern Clinical Psychiatry*. Philadelphia, London, Toronto: W. B. Saunders, 1973.

Korn, Wendy. "How Stress Affects Your Looks." *Ladies' Home Journal*, November 1983, p. 62.

Kotulak, Ronald. "Cry Your Neurotransmitters Out." *Honolulu Advertiser*, 1/1/84, p. A13.

Kozuki, Jules. "Against Aging: SOD, RNA, GH_3: The Cell Protectors." *Vim and Vigor Nutrition News*. Not dated.

Krentz, D. "Drawn and Repelled by Terrifying Love." *Sunday Star Bulletin and Advertiser*, 12/6/81.

Kunz, Jeffrey, editor. *The AMA Family Medical Guide*. New York: Random House, 1982.

Ladies' Home Journal, February 1983, p. 71.

Lake, Alice. "Alcoholism: Suddenly It's a Young Woman's Problem." *Redbook*, June 1982, p. 77.

LaMott, Kenneth. *Escape from Stress*. New York: G. P. Putnam's Sons, 1975.

Lance, Kathryn. *Getting Strong*. Indianapolis: Bobbs-Merrill, 1978.

Lance, Kathryn. "What Sex Researchers Now Know." *Ladies' Home Journal*, November 1983, p. 74.

Leo, John. "The New Scarlet Letter." *Time*, 8/2/82, p. 62.

"Let's Put Our Heads Together." *Woman*, April 1983, p. 19.

Levy, Stephen, Ph.D. *Managing the Drugs in Your Life.* New York: McGraw-Hill, 1983.

Lingeman, Richard. "Hanging Together in Muncie, Indiana." *Psychology Today*, May 1981, p. 8.

Lowe, Marian, and Ruth Hubbard. "Sociobiology and Biosociology: Can Science Prove the Biological Basis for Sex Differences in Behavior?" *Genes and Gender.* New York: Guardian Press, 1979, p. 91.

Luna, David. *The Lean Machine.* Culver City, Colorado: Peace Press, 1980.

Maccoby, E., and C. Jacklin. *The Psychology of Sex Differences.* Stanford University Press, 1974.

McGrath, Peter. "Are Men Running Scared?" *Mademoiselle*, May 1982, p. 139.

McNear, Suzanne. "A Scientist Looks at Romantic Love." *Cosmopolitan*, March 1980, p. 246.

Magnuson, Ed. "The Ultimate Betrayal." *Time*, 9/5/83, p. 20.

Mange, Richard, M.D., Peter Johe, M.D., and O. William Dayton, M.D. *The Runner's Medical Guide.* New York: Simon & Schuster, 1979.

Masters, William, and Virginia Johnson. *Human Sexual Response.* Boston: Little, Brown, & Co., 1966.

"Men Top Women in Trying to Save Marriage." *Star*, 1/17/84, p. 33.

Meyer, Jean. "Guide to Family Nutrition." *Family Circle*, September 1975.

"Midlife Crisis: Is It Unavoidable?" Interview with Daniel Levinson, *U.S. News & World Report*, October 25, 1982, p. 73.

"Mind and Body," *Science Digest*, December 1981, p. 102.

"Mind and Body," *Science Digest*, December 1982, p. 90.

"Mind and Body," *Science Digest*, September 1983, p. 90.

"Mind and Body," *Science Digest*, January 1984, p. 82.

Mindell, Earl. *Vitamin Bible.* New York: Warner Books, 1979.

Mitchell, G., Ph.D. *Human Sex Differences: A Primatologist's Perspective.* New York: Van Nostrand Reinhold, 1981.

Monagan, David. "The Failure of Coed Sports." *Psychology Today*, March 1978, p. 58.

Money, John. *Love and Love Sickness*. Baltimore: Johns Hopkins University Press, 1980.

Money, John, and Anke A. Ehrhardt. *Man and Woman, Boy and Girl*. Baltimore and London: Johns Hopkins University Press, 1972, pp. 206–208.

Morgan, Brian, M.D. "Mood Swings." *Family Circle*, 8/2/83, p. 20.

Ms. February 1983.

Mueller, William Behr. "Hormones: Messengers of Life." *Bestways*, March 1981, p. 75.

Murphy, Cullen. "Men and Women: How Different Are They?" *Saturday Evening Post*, October 1983, p. 48.

Murray, Frank, and Ruth Adams. *Program Your Heart for Health*. New York: Larchmont Books, 1977.

Murray, Frank, and Ruth Adams: *The Vitamin B_6 Book*. New York: Larchmont Books, 1980.

Murray, Linda. "The Sex Drive: Cycles of Desire." *Cosmopolitan*, April 1980, p. 261.

Nardi, Bonnie. Review of *Female Power and Male Dominance: On the Origin of Sexual Inequality* by Peggy Sunday (New York: Cambridge University Press, 1981), in *Sex Roles: A Journal of Research*, Vol. 8, No. 1, November 1982, pp. 1157–1160.

National Data Book and Guide to the Sources. U.S. Department of Commerce, Bureau of the Census, 1981.

National Institute of Education, 1975, quoted in Bird, Caroline, *What Women Want* (Houston, Texas: November 1977), p. 106.

"The Nearness of You." "Social Behavior," *Human Behavior*, May 1978, p. 27.

"News of Medicine." *Reader's Digest*, February 1983, p. 31.

Nollen, Stanley. *Network Schedules in Practice*. New York: Van Nostrand Reinhold, 1982.

Norman, Margie. "The Sexes." "Crosstalk," *Psychology Today*. December 1983, p. 70.

"The Nutrition Connection." *Let's Live*, October 1981.

Nutrition News. Pomona, California: Vol. IV, No. 8, 1981.

Offit, Adodah. "What Is Love?" *Cosmopolitan*, September 1981.

Oman, Anne H. "Washington Update." *Family Circle*, 6/19/84, p. 175.

Oppenheim, Mike, M.D. "Emotional Problems, Don't Be So Sure." *Woman's Day*, 3/8/83, p. 24.

O'Reilly, Jane. "Wife Beatings: The Silent Crime." *Time*, 9/5/83, p. 23.

"Parade Hotline," "Your Health." *Parade Magazine*, 6/29/80, p. 23.

Parlee, Mary Brown. "The Sexes Under Scrutiny: From Old Bias to New Theories." *Psychology Today*, November 1978, p. 62.

Pascoe, Jean. "Sex Hormones: What They Can Do and Cannot Do for You." *Woman's Day*, February 1971, p. 22.

Peplau, Letitia, Zick Rubin, and Charles Hill. "The Sexual Balance of Power." *Psychology Today*, November 1976, p. 142.

Pine, Devera. "Tootsie: From Dustin to Dorothy." *Health*, July 1983, p. 24.

Pogrebin, Letty Cottin. "A Conversation with Pollster Daniel Yankelovich." *Ms.*, July/August 1982, p. 140.

"Polymyalgia Rheumatica." *The Harvard Medical School Healthletter*, September 1983, Vol. VIII, No. 11.

Porter, Sylvia. "You and Your Money: The Truth about Equal Pay." *Ladies' Home Journal*, August 1982, p. 22.

Psychology Today: January 1978
May 1981
November 1981
December 1981
January 1983
January 1984.

Renwick, Patricia, Edward Lawler, and the *Psychology Today* staff. "What You Really Want from Your Job." *Psychology Today*, May 1978, p. 53.

Reynolds, Ann. *News*, Radio "99," 5:45 P.M., 11/25/83.

Reynolds, Bill. *Weight Training for Beginners*. Chicago: Contemporary Books, 1982.

Riddel, Rhoda. "Writing Personalities." *Human Behavior*, July 1978, p. 18.

"Right Now," *McCall's*, May 1979, p. 70.

"Right Now," *McCall's*, August 1982, p. 46.

Robinson, Bryan, Patsy Skeen, and Carol Flake-Hobson. "Sex-Stereotyped Attitudes of Male and Female Child Care Workers: Support for Androgynous Child Care." *Child Care Quarterly*, Vol. 9, No. 4, Winter 1980.

Ross, Susan Deller, and Ann Barcher. *The Rights of Women. An American Civil Liberties Handbook.* Toronto, London, Sydney, New York: Bantam Books, 1983.

Ross, Walter. "The Olympics: Unfair to Women." *Reader's Digest,* November 1983, p. 19.

Rothenberg, Robert E., M.D. *Medical Dictionary and Health Manual.* New York: New American Library, 1975.

Rubin, Debra. "Fifth Annual Salary Survey." *Working Woman,* February 1984, p. 59.

Rubin, Zick. "Reagan's Problem Women." *Psychology Today,* November 1982, p. 12.

Rubin, Zick. "The Love Research." *Human Behavior,* February 1977, p. 56.

Rubinstein, Carlin. "Survey Report, Money and Self-Esteem, Relationships, Secrecy, Envy, Satisfaction." *Psychology Today,* May 1981, p. 29.

Rubinstein, Carlin. "Real Men Don't Earn Less than Their Wives." *Psychology Today,* November 1982, p. 36.

Rubinstein, Carlin. "Wellness Is All." *Psychology Today,* p. 28.

Safran, Claire. "Hidden Lessons." *Parade Magazine,* 10/9/83, p. 12.

Sandler, Leonard. "Fat Cat Pay Depends on Slim Figures." *The Examiner,* 2/22/83, p. 29.

Sanford, Linda Tschirhart. *The Silent Children.* New York: McGraw-Hill, 1982.

Sanoff, Alvin. "19 Million Singles: Their Joys and Frustrations." *U.S. News & World Report,* 2/21/83, p. 53.

Scarf, Maggie. "The Promiscuous Woman." *Psychology Today,* July 1980, p. 78.

Schumann, Wendy. "The Violent American Way of Life." *Parents Magazine,* September 1980.

Science Digest, May 1982, p. 99.

Science Digest, July 1982, p. 96.

Science Digest, October 1982, p. 98.

Scott, Walter. "Personality Parade," *Parade Magazine,* 1/1/84, p. 2.

Scott, Walter. "Personality Parade," *Parade Magazine,* 1/8/84.

Segal, Jules. "The Sexes' Little Differences." *Health,* July, 1983, p. 28.

Selden, Gary. "Frailty, Thy Name's Been Changed." *Ms.,* July, 1981.

Serbin, Lisa, and L. K. Daniel O'Leary. "How Nursery Schools Teach Girls to Shut Up." *Psychology Today*, December, 1975, p. 56.

SerVaas, Cory, M.D. "As the Twig Is Bent." *Saturday Evening Post*, February 1984, p. 62.

"Sex and the Older Woman." *Health and Longevity Report*, 9/15/83, Vol. 2, No. 1, p. 3.

"Sex Problems We Don't Talk About and Should." *Redbook*, February 1980, p. 27.

Sexton, Patricia Cayo. "Schools Are Emasculating Our Boys." *Psychology and Personal Growth*. Abe Arkoff, editor. Boston: Allyn and Bacon, 1975.

Shearer, Lloyd. "Intelligence Report," *Parade Magazine*, 1/16/83, p. 12.

Shearer, Lloyd. "Intelligence Report," *Parade Magazine*, 2/20/83, p. 10.

Shearer, Lloyd. "Intelligence Report," *Parade Magazine*, 7/31/83.

Shearer, Lloyd. "Intelligence Report," *Parade Magazine*, 12/25/83, p. 8.

Siber, Sherman. *The Male*. New York: Charles Scribner's Sons, 1981.

Silva, John, III. "An Evaluation of Fear of Success in Female, Male, and Non-Athletes." *Journal of Sports Psychology*, Vol. 4, No. 1, 1982.

Simonds, John, M.D., and Humberto Parraga, M.D. "Prevalence of Sleep Disorders and Sleep Behaviors in Children and Adolescents." *Journal of the American Academy of Child Psychiatry*, Vol. 21, No. 4, July 1982, pp. 383–388.

Smith, Jeanne, M.D. *Instant Medical Adviser*. Mundelein, Ill.: Mundelein Career Institute, 1970.

"Social Behavior." *Human Behavior*, June 1977, p. 32.

"Sociobiology." *Science Digest*, July 1982, p. 64.

"Some Men's Work Is Never Done." *McCall's*, February 1982, p. 76.

Somerville, Elaine. "A Champion of America's Old Women." *Modern Maturity*, October/November 1983, pp. 112, 113.

Spangler, E., et al. "Token Women: An Empirical Test of Kanter's Hypothesis." *American Journal of Sociology*, 84, pp. 160–170.

Squires, Sally. "Go Ahead and Have a Good Cry: It's Healthy." *Honolulu Star Bulletin*, 8/30/82, p. B3.

Star. "College Women Admire Brains Not Brawn," 1/24/84, p. 7.

———. "Now Men Are Complaining of Sex Harassment," 6/21/83, p. 19.

Starr, Bernard, Ph.D., and Marcella Weiner, Ph.D. *The Starr-Weiner Report on Sex and Sexuality in the Mature Years*. New York: Stein and Day, 1981.

Statistical Abstract of the U.S.A. Census, 1981, 102d Edition. U.S. Department of the Census.

Stewart, Kirk, and Aaron Rosenblatt. "Woman's 1984 Contribution to Social Work Journals." *Social Work*, 25, pp. 204–209.

Stump, Jane. "A Wellness Handbook" (unpublished manuscript).

"Suddenly It's a Young Woman's Problem." *Redbook*, June 1982, p. 77.

Symons, Donald. "He Versus She." *Science Digest*, December 1983, p. 86.

Tavris, Carol. "Men and Women Report Their Views on Masculinity." *Psychology Today*, January 1977, p. 35.

Tavris, Carol, and Susan Sadd. *The Redbook Report on Female Sexuality*. New York: Dell Books, 1977.

Thatcher, Michael. "Personal File." *Human Behavior*, November 1978, p. 12.

Tobias, Sheila, and Shelah Leader. "An Intelligent Woman's Guide to the Military Mind." *Ms.*, August 1982, p. 118.

Ubell, Earl. "Health on Parade." *Parade Magazine*, 2/13/83, p. 13.

United States Census, 1980.

"Update." *Science Digest*, September 1981.

U.S.A. Today. "Life Today." 6/7/83, p. 1.

Van De Velde, T. H. *Ideal Marriage: Its Physiology and Technique*. New York: Random House, 1966.

Wagenvoord, James, and Peyton Bailey. *Women: A Book for Men*, 1979. *Men: A Book for Women*, 1978. New York: Avon.

Wallis, Claudia. "Stress, Can We Cope?" *Time*, 6/6/83, p. 48.

Weeborn, Elizabeth. "Some Men's Work Is Never Done." "Right Now," *McCall's*, February 1983, p. 83.

Weekes, C. *British Medical Journal*, 2:469, 1973.

Wetzeteon, Ross. "What Do Men and Women Really Want in Bed Besides Each Other?" *Mademoiselle*, July 1981.

What Everyone Should Know About Cancer. Greenfield, Massachusetts: Channing Bete Company, 1978.

What Everyone Should Know About Depression. Greenfield, Massachusetts: Channing Bete Company, 1978.

White, David. "Pursuit of the Ultimate Aphrodisiac." *Psychology Today,* September 1981, p. 9.

Wilder, Rachael. "Sexual Choice, The Female's Newly Discovered Role." *Science Digest,* March 1982, p. 84.

Willis, Ellen. "The Politics of Dependency." *Ms.,* August 1982, p. 181.

Willis, Judith. "How Many More Nights in a Row Won't I Sleep?" *Woman's Magazine,* April 1983, p. 37.

Wilmore, Jack H. "Hypokinetic Disease: Are You a Victim?" *Shape,* December 1981, p. 75.

Wilson, E. O. "Human Decency in Animals." *The New York Times Magazine,* 10/12/75, p. 50.

Winter, Richard, M.D. *Executive Fitness.* New York: McGraw-Hill, 1983.

Woman's Body. New York: A Bantam Book, 1977.

"Women's Double Dose of Immunity." *Science Digest,* September 1982, p. 90.

"Work." *Human Behavior,* January 1979, p. 34.

World Almanac and Book of Facts 1981. New York: The Honolulu Advertiser Newspaper Enterprise Association, Inc., 1981.

World Almanac and Book of Facts 1984. New York: The Newspaper Enterprise Association, Inc., 1984.

"Worthy of Note." *Modern Maturity,* December 1981-January 1982, p. 12.

Yalow, Rosalyn. "Men and Women Are Not the Same." *The New York Times,* 1/31/82, p. E23.

You and Your Blood Pressure. Greenfield, Massachusetts: Channing Bete Company, 1978.

You and Your Heart. New York: American Heart Association, 1970.

"Your Health." "Parade Hotline," *Parade Magazine,* 6/29/80, p. 24.

"Your Inner Alarm Clock." "Mind and Body," *Science Digest,* January 1982, p. 101.

Zigli, Barbara. "U.S.A. School Boards Now 37% Women." *U.S.A. Today,* 1/24/84.

Zimbardo, Philip, O. Paul Pilkonis, and Robert Norwood. "The Social Disease Called Shyness." *Psychology Today*, May 1975, p. 69–72.
Zimmerman, Dave. "We'd Work Even If We Were Rich." *U.S.A. Today*, 1/24/84.